HEATHERS

AND HEATHLANDS

CHRIS HOWKINS

Published by
Chris Howkins

1

COPYRIGHT

© Text and Illustrations Chris Howkins 2004

ISBN 1 901087 50 6

PUBLISHER
Chris Howkins, 70 Grange Road,
New Haw, Addlestone, Surrey,
KT15 3RH

PRINTED
Hobbs the Printers Ltd.,
Brunel Road,
Southampton,
Hampshire.
SO40 3WX

CONDITIONS OF SALE
This book is sold subject to the
condition that it shall not, by
way of trade or otherwise be
circulated in any form of binding
or cover other than that in which
it is published and without a
similar condition including this
condition being imposed upon
the subsequent purchaser.

ALL RIGHTS RESERVED
No part of this publication may be
reproduced, stored in a retrieval system,
or transmitted in any form or by any
means electronic, mechanical,
photocopying, recording or otherwise,
without the prior permission of the publisher.

Ling

Cover photograph
by Robert McGibbon
Calluna, Erica and Ulex

CONTENTS

INTRODUCTION

People have given our heathlands an amazing history, stretching back over 4,000 years. How could they earn a living throughout the year, from so few different plants, on such poor soils? That question led to a review of the uses of the plants, published as the *Heathland Harvest* back in 1997. The book is now out of print so parts of it, primarily the chapters on heathers, both *Calluna* and *Ericas*, have been extracted, revised and enlarged, into this volume, together with other relevant material. This time, more material has been included to reveal the ways of life of the heathlanders, who exploited the plants and the landscape to satisfy their daily needs. This falls into two phases: firstly the feudal days of a manor when people lived in the villages and hamlets and went out to work the heath just as they did the fields, and secondly, the later phase, when land had gone into private ownership and people were marginalised onto the heathlands to eke out as good a living as they could get. Included also is material on the modern efforts to conserve these great historic landscapes. The final chapter endeavours to draw together this diverse material into an overall view *but* remember other valuable plants - Bracken, Furze, Birch - are missing from this volume. They will be reviewed again in due course.

Names are a problem with these shrubs, since they all get called *heather*. The Common Heather or Ling, *Calluna vulgaris*, is the important species in English ethnobotany and the bulk of this book deals with that shrub exclusively. It will be referred to as Ling, for simplicity and clarity, except in quotations, which are kept faithful to the original. There should be no confusion since species of the genus *Erica* are not reviewed until the end of this book. These language problems are hundreds of years old. The word 'heather' comes to us from Middle English but derives ultimately from the Germanic (Saxon) language. The name 'ling' on the other hand came with the Vikings and is from the Norse languages. In old medical writings we encounter names like 'she-heather' and 'he-heather', reflecting separate herbal treatments for the gender of the patient. Most frequently she-heather referred to the *Ericas* and he-heather to *Calluna*. Obviously there could have been a large margin of error between these two when being gathered and used; luckily neither are toxic! In modern times any species gets called 'heath', especially in horticultural writings, but is avoided here as it is too imprecise and causes additional confusion when the word is used to describe the landscape. Thus the longer 'heathland' has been used in this book for the landscape. It is an ecological term. It has a different meaning from 'common' which is a legal/administrative term. Some heathlands are, or were, commons, while other landscapes such as downland, woodland and even the seashore, have also been commons. These are areas over which specified people had specified rights, known in general English as 'commoners' rights'.

The notion of 'rights' implies the existence of 'wrongs' and the court records make all too clear that this distinction was not lost upon our forebears. Today, sadly, there are those who start screaming about commoners' rights as though they were a licence to behave at will. Such a luxury never existed. The commons were worked under the aegis of the manor courts for the common good of the community, not to satisfy private greed or wishes. That too becomes abundantly clear in the court records when landowners tried to enclose commons to the exclusion of those holding commoners' rights over it. On the whole, such rights have been annulled on most heathlands today but with some notable exceptions - the feral livestock grazing the New Forest for example. They are not only an important part of the local agricultural economy but make a considerable contribution to the local tourist industry too. Other traditional grazing sites still in use are scattered from West Wales to Ashdown Forest in East Sussex. Recent conservation measures have reintroduced grazing to some heaths, giving us the additional benefit of a view into the past. What a past it has been too! Time to explore it......

Thanks are due to Dr. Robert McGibbon for his professional advice throughout and for the cover photograph, to Aaron Mason for putting the book together and to Janet Blight for the use of her drawings on p.76 (right) and p.79.

PREHISTORIC BEGINNINGS

There are now two explanations for the origins of the landscape that we call 'heathland'. The explanation of longest standing has them being developed at the end of the Stone Age when man first started farming. He changed from a livelihood dependant upon hunting, gathering and fishing to one supplemented with animal husbandry and crop-growing, that would eventually become dominant. The period and culture of the first farmers is called Neolithic. Big changes were ahead as man discovered metallurgy techniques and stone tools were replaced by ones of bronze - the Bronze Age had arrived. It was during these times that it was necessary to clear woodland to increase the amount of grazing available and to make way for small fields.

The woodlands they cleared had been making a world of their own, holding in moisture, shielding off direct sun, rain, frost and winds, while continually recycling nutrients, with each autumn's leaf fall. Once the trees have been cleared all that system has gone. The woodland plants do not colonise the space again because it is too exposed for them. It has lost its humid atmosphere and soil moisture dries out rapidly. It does, however, suit many species of grasses and it was these that colonised, to increase the grazing for the new livestock and to attract wild herbivores that man still hunted. Some new clearances were made into fields, where cereal grasses were grown. They did well in the humus rich soil of the former woodland but soon the soil was exhausted, especially on the acid sands, the 'hungry' soils. Man moved on and with more slash-and-burn, cleared more trees and started again. The abandoned plots on the acid sandy soils were colonised by a special group of plants that could withstand full expose to the elements and grow successfully in soils with low nutrient levels. These are the species we would now think of as heathland plants, including the *Calluna*, and thus these became the first heathlands.

There are a couple of problems with this familiar scenario. Firstly, when we read, time and again, that in this way, heathlands are 'man made' this blinds us to the landscape of the Late Stone Age.

The plants that colonised, such as the *Calluna*, had to come from somewhere - there *were* patches of *natural* heathland in existence. The coasts had Ling and we can still see it today. It scrambles down the cliffs of acidic rock where it's long woody roots prize their way into cracks and faults, greedy for any nutrient it can find. The sea birds of the cliffs add some more, through their droppings, through the rotting remains of their catches and even calcium from their eggshells. For moisture, in addition to rain, there is the run-off from the land behind, which on occasions floods the gullies. Ling has adapted to this too, just as on the heathlands it can tolerate standing in water for weeks where the iron pans in the soil impede drainage. At the same time, it has to be tolerant of drought. Thus it has tiny leaves to reduce the amount of water that can be lost by transpiration, and even these little leaves are rolled backwards to enclose the under-surface where the breathing holes would be exposed to the drying wind. Even the insides of these rolled-up leaves are festooned with little hairs to trap moisture and reduce losses. Back in prehistoric times, the *Calluna* proved well-adapted to move inland from cliffs, sandy beaches and dunes, to colonise the acidic sandy wastes of deserted fields. The natural reserves of coastal Ling are still there, helping to give parts of Cornwall it's famous beauty. Even in the south east there are still small examples on the cliffs at Hastings and Fairlight.

The second problem with the usual story of the formation of heathlands is that of the farmers continually moving on to a fresh site whenever their crops had exhausted the soils in their fields. This is grossly simplified and makes the people sound almost nomadic and their farming very ad hoc. Now that 'landscape archaeology' and heathlands are both enjoying a high profile we have archaeologists rushing out after a heathland fire to look at the blackened ground. It is the first time they've been able to see it, since bracken and Ling had hitherto clothed the surface from view. Now they are finding more and more Bronze Age field boundaries - the remains of the enclosing banks. That's very intriguing. Why did the little communities build these banks? Was it to raise the depth of soil so that a palisade could be driven in to the top to keep animals from eating the crops? Were they to define property, implying communal

*Bronze Age men's fashion options
included longer clothing for bad
weather, a tunic that belted under
the armpits, or trousers. Leather
shoes could be changed for boots
or even gaiters with two buttons
at the side. The amber necklace
shown was an optional extra.*

decision making as to who could have land and how much and exactly where? Building the banks was a demanding task so they were obviously important. They imply levels of social organisation that people have been slow to credit to our ancient forebears. Interestingly, they reveal that early agriculture really did degrade the soil: archaeological excavations have found the earlier richer soil layer *underneath* the later banks or a poor heathland type soil.

This traditional view of developments sees the landscape taking a long time to become so extensive. However, there is now a second explanation, based upon recent work, edited by F. W. M. Vera, and published as *Grazing Ecology and Forest History*. This challenges the traditional view of the great Wildwood covering everywhere. Instead, it reasons a prehistoric landscape of broken woodland cover, with grassy areas *and heathlands*. Initially, many people found this a very radical concept but now wise heads, in differing disciplines, are nodding sagely. Certainly it explains the wide distribution of *Calluna* more convincingly than having it spread inland from the coasts. That would have been a secondary movement.

Archaeologists believe the expansion of heathlands began in East Anglia 5,000 years ago. Many heaths are thought to be 4,500 to 4,000 years old, while others are some 3,000 years old, or much younger. Thus the early heathlands were being created by the same peoples who worked on the succeeding versions of Stonehenge. That is a monument we treasure as a World Heritage Site yet we don't know how it was used. We *do* know how their heathlands were used and have continued with many of the practices until the present day.

LING TURVES

Turf nowadays suggests grass, whether for lawns or in a sporting context. Another of its meanings has been sods of Ling cut from the heathlands. These were primarily for fuel but were used also for roofing, walling and insulating root clamps against frost. It is one case where 'heath' and 'common' could in effect be the same, for cutting turf was one of the commoners' rights - the right of *turbary*, from the Latin *turba* for turf. It was being documented in this name by the 13th century and the right was formalised in the Law of Turbary of 1567. However, the practice must be of prehistoric origin and it lasted until the coming of the railways, bringing cheap coal. Even then some of the poorest families continued with turves and in some places the practice was revived during the fuel shortages of the Second World War (e.g. they were cut on The Flashes, Frensham, Surrey). There is an unexpected connection with paving because flagstones or flags derive from the Norse *flaga* meaning cut turves. This is still current on Dartmoor where turves are called *vags*.

The turves themselves were the matted roots and ground litter of the Ling. Today stands of Ling are often dotted with birch, pine, gorse and tussocks of grasses but most of these would have been harvested or grazed out in former times. Ideally the plants needed to be young with short twiggy growth, as this was mirrored below ground with a mat of fibrous roots that bound the turf together. As the Ling ages and the stems become woodier so too do the roots and then the turves fall to pieces. This landscape of short massed Ling is rarely seen today, on a large scale, but persisted into the age of photography and post cards. The Ling landscape was like that because of grazing (and because tall material was cut for brooms and thatching). Thus using the heathland as a grazing site pruned the Ling to produce matted turves for use as fuel, at the same time. However, this created a conflict of interest in some areas. Taking too much Ling for fuel left too little to feed the livestock. That's before the needs of the thatcher and broom-maker are taken into consideration. The manorial courts had to balance out these conflicts, in relation to whatever other resources their lands might provide. For example, they might have enough straw or reed beds to do without Ling for thatching. Always it was a balanced judgement between the community's needs and their resources with which to fulfil them. Consequently a single history of the heathlands cannot possibly be written; each manor had its own version.

It was in May, June and July that the turves were cut. The manors must have tried to do that as early as possible to leave the men free for haymaking during June and July. Otherwise it must have been done immediately afterwards, before the corn harvest. July was the wettest month of the year for long periods in history and that was no help for haymaking so maybe if rain interrupted that harvest they turned to cutting turves instead. All the turves had to be turned over to dry, as they were cut. The drying process was important if the turves were to shrink tightly together and burn well. Apart from that, the best turves came from the wettest parts of the heath where the acid water delayed the processes of decay, so allowing thicker layers of 'peat' to build up. Those turves made the best fuel and wet districts became renowned for them, like Aldershot in Hampshire and Frimley in Surrey. After drying they were carted home and stacked for winter use, providing somebody had not stolen them in the meantime. They were vital to the local economy and therefore very desirable, making theft a real threat. One example may be read in the *Deposition Book* of Richard Wyatt,[1] Justice of the Peace at Kingston-upon-Thames, who in August 1722 found John Portsmouth before him. He had gone out onto the common at Egham and carted off a load of turves cut by John Watts, a local labourer. News of this got to Watts who reached the site in time to accost Portsmouth coming back for a second load. Portsmouth announced that he'd take what he liked off the common. Watts knew his rights and turned to the law.

Cutting was performed with a spade designed specifically for the job but that design varied from district to district. A common version had a stout cross bar to the handle upon which the worker could throw his weight in order to cut through the roots. The blade was somewhat heart-shaped and fixed to the handle at an angle appropriate for a good stomach thrust! The whole tool is unusually heavy, to help do the job, but lighter versions have been seen in museum collections, some without the cross-bar top, some with a cutting flange. To use any other tool could be an offence; there was a penalty of ten shillings per offender levied in the Dorset manor of Moreton, according to the Court Books of 1810. Each turf measured about nine inches wide and twice as long. As for the thickness, it has been recorded at three-quarters of an inch but this proved difficult to achieve when tested. It was so thin the turf fell apart, yet on many heathlands that is about all that exists to slice off the underlying sand. As with so many seemingly simple country tasks, turf-cutting benefits from a considerable input of experience and practised dexterity.

Stripping the turves off the sand by the thousand would soon have created a useless desert but long ago our ancestors learned how to maintain the resource. They took out every third turf in a row and staggered the rows to create a (distorted) chequer board effect. Thus each of the thousands of turves was cut separately rather than cutting a long strip and chopping it into sections. This left sandy patches surrounded by turf and therefore less exposed to erosion. The Ling soon grew back and was ready for cutting again in six or seven years. That meant that a household taking 5,000 turves on a seven-year rotation would need nearly an acre of heathland. When losses due to rocks, tree, shrubs etc. are taken into account then the estimate becomes even closer to an acre, except of course they were taking only every third turf, so a total of three acres was needed. Surely fuel must have been a prime, limiting factor in the development of those heathland communities that never expanded for generation upon generation. It is a factor rarely commented upon. Indeed it is rare to find anybody even enquiring why the little communities did not expand.

Cutting too many turves created arid 'desert' conditions. Once the weather had destroyed the soil structure and created loose sand it was almost impossible to stabilise it again for plant regrowth. A well-known example is the sandy 'beach' that tourists created by erosion beside Frensham Great Pond in Surrey. It must have been back in the late 1950s that a section was first fenced off to allow it to recover. It didn't. Peat was added to see if that would aid plant growth. It didn't. Next they tried spent hops from the local brewery and again it failed. There was still more sand than anything else in the late 1960s. It has recovered now but the time interval would have been disastrous if the local community had been dependent upon that land. That side of the pond still has incredible deep loose sand where visitors are permitted access en masse. It is an impressive example of what happens if the soil is abused.

Over-exploitation *did* occur in the past. Those periods of long icy winters drove people to cut extra turf, with disastrous results. It happened at Bagshot, Surrey, judging by the writing of Daniel Defoe on his *Tour Through The Whole Island of Great Britain* in the 1720s. He did not like heathlands to start with and described Bagshot Heath as "*a mark of the just resentment showed by Heaven upon the Englishman's pride; I mean the pride they show in boasting of their country, its fruitfulness, pleasantness, richness, the fertility of the soil, &c. whereas here is a vast tract of land, some of it within seventeen or eighteen miles of the capital city; which is not only poor, but even quite sterile, given up to barrenness, horrid and frightful to look on, not only good for little, but good for nothing.*"

He goes on to tell us, indirectly, that the Ling had been over-exploited for "*I was so far in danger of smothering with the clouds of sand, which were raised by the storm, that I could neither keep it out of my mouth, nose or eyes; and when the wind was over, the sand appeared spread over the adjacent fields of the forest some miles distant, so that it ruins the very soil.*" He did appreciate that "*This sand indeed is checked by the heath or heather, which grows in it.*"[2]

Over forty of our larger moths use the Ling as a larval food plant.

TURVES FOR FUEL

The homes of the heathlands were very small single storey structures, built of turves. Despite their smallness, they required, ideally, at least 4,000-5,000 turves per winter for fuel. Isn't it difficult to imagine a stack that size and the work that went into making it. Records from the New Forest show some allocations were as high as 6,000 but the same records reveal many were as low as 2,000,[3] so don't imagine families sitting cosily round a fragrant peaty fire all winter. Shortage of supplies must have made theft a serious temptation. The heat given off from the smouldering turves was steady and long lasting but rather gentle. It was inadequate for even boiling a pot or kettle, so it had to be boosted for bringing them to the boil. For this a 'hurrier' was added, such as a handful of dried Furze or dead Bracken. These materials themselves were valued for other purposes and must have been used sparingly. Life was never easy.

Turves could be bought so obviously some people cut them to earn part of their living. In later times this could imply that people with rights of turbary were sufficiently affluent to be able to afford coal and could therefore sell off their own quota of turf. Some of the new private landowners who had enclosed the commons could also have been selling off turves to the poor who had them by right formerly. They cost, in the first couple of decades of the 19th century, seven shillings per thousand, when a labourer's weekly wage might be eleven shillings. Parishes like Pirbright, Surrey, have records of turves being given to the poor as alms.

The system was not restricted to the countryside; townsfolk had rights of turbary too. The townsfolk of Poole, Dorset, had rights to cut turf on Canford Common. Similarly, the townsfolk of Wareham, also in Dorset, obviously had similar rights as it was hot turf ashes thrown on a dung heap that caused the famous and highly destructive fire in the town in 1762. From Stowborough School at Wareham, comes the unusual record that the headmaster was allowed to take 10,000 turves a year off Stoborough Common.[4] Townsfolk could buy turves, in the markets local to the heathlands, such as Swanage

for the Purbeck heathlands.[5] At Poole there was a demand from
industry, in the 17th century, when turves fired the furnaces in the
Earl of Huntingdon's copperas and alum works. Indeed, this was so
important to him that he enclosed the heathland to preclude local
people exercising their rights of turbary but they tore down his
fences and won their case against him in court.[6]

Ultimately turf became the fuel of the very poor but with little
else to burn it was highly valued. It became of great social
consequence during the period of the Enclosure Acts of the 18th and
early 19th centuries when traditional cutting grounds went suddenly
into private ownership. Many parishes, already straining to maintain
the poor, made new fuel arrangements, as in Middlesex at Charlton
and Sunbury-on-Thames where a new Charity was created. It set
aside 46 acres of heathland to continue fuelling the poor after the
Enclosure Award of 1800. By the time Gertrude Jekyll published her
Old West Surrey in 1904 she viewed turf cutting as a 'privilege'.

ROOFING TURVES

Turf roofs do not survive long, especially in the south-east where
the annual rainfall is comparatively low. The expectancy is extended
in wetter regions by allowing grass to grow over them to bind them
together. For this to prosper the pitch of the roof is crucial and the
rainfall must be adequate. Although there are scattered references to
such roofs in the south there is a dearth of information about them.
There are just a few photographs of them. Of those seen, all seem to
be associated with the Arts and Crafts Movement, which was centred
upon Haslemere, amid the adjoining heathlands of Surrey,
Hampshire and West Sussex. The Movement only began at the very
end of the 19th century, by which time the railways had been
bringing cheap materials into Haslemere for over a generation. Thus
there is an element of doubt as to how accurately practices were
revived, even though many did persist in the local countryside.
Some photographs certainly raise doubt and questions.

Trotter went so far as to say, *"Considered realistically, the movement seems in retrospect a belated and futile attempt, by a bunch of middle-class cranks, to roll back the Industrial Revolution. But at the time, it must have inspired its adherents with a sense of doing something worthwhile, and it did bring them into contact with some of the working people of the countryside, who were largely ignored by the rest of the immigrant intelligentsia."*[7]

Of the photographs seen, none revealed clearly how the turves were laid. It would seem reasonable that they should overlap, like stone tiles, such as the 'Horsham slabs' still to be seen on the roof of the parish church at nearby Witley. The difficulty with this, however, would be bonding the overlaps together when there were the bases of Ling plants between them. Thus it is not altogether surprising that in some photographs it looks as though the turves were butted side by side. That raises a different problem. They would not have been waterproof, since the peaty content would shrink in dry weather, leaving gaps. Furthermore, the pitch of the roof does not look right. Then there is the question of which way up the turves were laid. That is very clear. They were laid twig side upwards, because the twigs have not been cut off. That surely casts considerable doubt over authenticity. Originally the people living under such a roof would have been too poor to waste those twigs. They would have been cut off for fuel. Even the roofer in Scotland, where there was a far greater chance of the Ling living on, sheared off the untidy bits to finish the job. Also, such twigs would trap an extra depth of snow, increasing the weight on what may well have been poor quality roofing timbers. Not surprisingly then, very poor quality roofs were noted by writers in the past.

THATCHING

Although thatching today is almost exclusively done with reeds or straw, there was a wider range of materials in the past, including such heathland plants as Furze, Bracken and Ling. A detailed description of thatching with Ling in the southern counties proved elusive, when the *Heathland Harvest* was first written, and no such account has come to light since. There *are* thatchers who can still use it but they are rare. There is a number of Internet sites lamenting the way modern heather roofs fail to keep out the rain. However, leaks may not be due necessarily to poor skills. The way the Ling was harvested and the pitch of the roof both have their part to play.

The most detailed description found was that of John Collier for a competition in 1831[8] but that was for Scotland. It should therefore be treated with caution since thatching techniques have regional variations. However, the skills have been developed since prehistoric times and therefore have certain basic and long-established principles that are worthy of note. At least this Scots writer was himself a thatcher and should have known what he was talking about, although his account raises as many questions as it answers.

Firstly, Mr Collier records an *increase* in its use at that time in Aberdeenshire as a result of improved thatching techniques. To modern readers, that implies that they changed the way they did it. In fact, he might be recording that roofs were once again being thatched 'properly' rather than patched. At the same time, he was no doubt being careful not to offend local landlords, who employed him. There had been a widespread practice of providing homes for tenants on short leases. Many were for a year only. Tenants therefore left the leaks for the next person to deal with, resulting in makeshift repairs and an overall decline in roofing. There comes a time when the whole roof is so patched and decayed that it *must* be stripped off and thatched afresh, if the landlord was to be left with a home to lease at all. Maybe Collier's statement reflects this. The increase may have been due to an additional factor. Sir Walter Scott (died the following year) had revived Scottish nationalism, and in many cases invented aspects that we now think of as being of ancient tradition. Anything inherently Scottish became fashionable and that may have led to a return to heather thatch.

Collier tells us it was the thatching technique, the quality of the Ling and the pitch of the roof that would determine ultimate lasting quality. The best was expected to last 20-30 years (comparable to straw thatch). The pitch for a building twelve feet across inside, needed to be six inches above the square. This increased by two inches for every extra foot of internal dimension. The best material was from dry sites where the Ling had been pulled (to leave a tuft a root) rather than cut. This could be done throughout the year but was avoided if possible between June and August when it was more sappy. Stems needed to be 18-20 inches long and unbranched. It was bound in sheaves and laid flat to compress it straight, as it dried out for three or four days. Once on the roof the Ling was sometimes held down against gales with 'rope-yarn' but was liable to be eaten through by rodents; in the south there are references to making rope out of the twisted stems of both Birch and Ling and maybe this was their purpose.

Thatch was applied sometimes directly on to the roof timbers but more often there was a basic covering of tiles or turf. He anticipates queries about using both tiles and thatch by explaining that the porous tiles absorbed one seventh of their dry weight in water, which then expanded and shattered the tiles during hard frosts, implying that the thatch was to keep them drier and to insulate them from the cold. Whether that was done in the southern counties I do not know but it is highly likely during those past decades when winters were so cold that Cedar of Lebanon, Weeping Willow and Walnut trees died and oxen were roasted on the frozen Thames.

Thatching began at the eaves and worked sideways in horizontal layers instead of the vertical strips he says he would have created for straw thatching. The first layer overhung the wall by a hand's breadth and the second layer overhung that, to create the eaves, which were trimmed off horizontally with a large knife to conclude the task. From the eaves, thatching progressed up the roof at the same pitch as the roof, working in blocks four feet wide, starting with the ladder two feet from the right end, and working from left to right. Then the ladder was moved to the left and another block was worked up, abutting that already positioned on the right. The two had to be carefully bonded. Once five layers had been added the ladder was repositioned over the eaves to allow for reaching further up the roof. The first, second, third, and fifth layers were bedded in clay: '*a sufficient quantity to make them adhere to each other*' since the eaves suffered most from exposure. Thereafter clay was used more sparingly, for every third layer. The turf or tiles beneath stopped the clay dropping through into the room. References from elsewhere, including the south, are to furze, bracken, rushes, straw and hay being do used. It sounds as though using the clay effectively and efficiently was where skill and experience came to the fore. An experienced eye and well-practised skill also sound crucial when we read that, '*in order to carry off the rain more readily, it is necessary to give the roof, or rather the rib, a little swell towards the middle,*' by using longer lengths of Ling. That must be a very ancient technique since it echoes the Viking way of doing it. It must have demanded skill and experience too, in order to avoid a hump! Once all the Ling stems had been laid, with their cut ends tilted 25-30 degrees upwards to accelerate run-off, then the ridge was sealed. For this a mixture of clay and chopped straw was packed into place. Finally '*The whole surface of the work ought then to be gone over with a pair of scissors* [shears], *cutting off only, however, the loose detached fibres.*'

The key to this all holding in place well must lie surely with the bonding of clay. That is why he wanted the roots left on if possible. A tuft of fibres would not pull out of the clay as readily as bare stems. Thus good Ling thatch was harvested by pulling rather than cutting. That is exactly what we find in such medieval records as those of 1353-4 for the manor of Thorner (Yorks) when the watermill was being repaired. They paid 2d for a cartload of 'lyng' for roofing the mill and 2d in wages for a man to uproot the lyng; 3d for hiring a cart to carry the lyng to the mill and 7½d in wages for the roofer to work three days thatching the mill with the lyng and straw.[9] Presumably the straw became the under-layer. There seems little reason to suppose such practices were not current in the southern counties. Heather thatch would not have been used on the poorest quality buildings since it required reasonable roofing woodwork; Ling is heavier than straw and rushes and might bring the lot down if it were cheap Poplar or Willow. Heather thatch is also said to be more inflammable that rushes and straw so perhaps it was avoided for any building with fires, such as bakehouses, which were built separate from the main buildings specifically to control the fire risk.

Admittedly more cereals were grown in the southern counties, putting more straw on the market, which might have been bought in preference. However, the uses of straw were legion so maybe it was not so readily available as we might imagine. Perhaps that is reflected in the financial accounts from medieval building sites. Normally construction work ceased for the winter. This was partly a financial saving since so many of the workmen were paid by the day, which was expensive in winter when there were so few hours of daylight. It was a practical expedient too, since bad weather, especially frost, destroys fresh mortar. Thus unfinished walls were thatched for the winter to protect them from the elements. Several different materials are accounted in the records. These included reeds, which were a high quality material, and presumably restricted most often to precious situations, such as incomplete cathedral vaults. Straw was much used; even pea haulm occurs, which surely implies a local shortage of anything better. Heather occurs too, as at Nottingham in 1369 when they bought five 'thraves' of it for this purpose.[10] In 1362 it is recorded for Windsor.[11] They bought 125 cartloads,[12] which would have cleared a very sizeable area of heathland. Perhaps providing such supplies became an important part of the economy of some heathland districts, adjacent to long-term building works. Thoughts go to the New Forest whence Winchester would have taken its main supplies. The city must have needed a massive amount every year throughout the Middle Ages, when there was always high status construction work in progress:- the castle, gateways and city walls, the bishop's castle, the cathedral, the college, all the monasteries and not forgetting St. Cross a mile outside. When most building work ceased for the winter the city's population must have dropped dramatically. We can imagine those permanent residents who were so dependent in their varying ways upon the summer influx, viewed such carts of Ling as the final note that rang-in the cold winter months ahead. Within a few days all would seem as quiet as the frost in the Itchen water meadows beyond the walls.

As for the landscape that yielded such material - that is a different matter. To get the tall straight unbranching stems with roots requires thickets of seedlings that are close-growing to draw them up tall to the light and retard side-branching. That can occur if stands of Ling have been cleared to ground level or are regenerating as seedlings following a fire. If small amounts were needed to thatch a wall then many heathlands could have provided that by cutting selectively the best stems. Of course, such stems would not be there if the site were grazed regularly. It is more evidence pointing to the likelihood that areas of heathland were given specific designations, with areas set-aside to grow on into the tall material needed by thatchers and broom-makers.

Meadow Pipit, known formerly in some districts as the "Ling Bird"

BROOM-MAKING

Back in the 18th century, when Linnaeus was organising plant names into the form we use today, he named the Ling, *Calluna*, from the Greek *kallunein*, meaning 'to sweep'. Even then the plant was famous for broom-making. Unlike many rural occupations, that of broom-making appears separately in many documents, and so we can piece together something of their story. For example, back in 1769, on 15th February, Joseph Ellis and Sarah Cooper were busy cutting Ling on Byfleet Common, in Surrey. Soon they'd got the cuttings bundled up and loaded on to their donkey which Sarah then led down to the king's highway and turned right for Weybridge, leaving Joe to carry on cutting. Suddenly her way was blocked by two other broom-makers, Thomas and Henry Woods, intent upon hi-jacking her load. They hadn't taken into account how loudly Sarah could yell, so as Thomas "*stopped the ass and threw down the heath*" so Joe arrived on the scene. The Woods brothers turned on him and "*violently beat and wounded him.*" He, knowing his rights, turned to the law officers. Thus we are able to read this story in the *Deposition Book* of Richard Wyatt, Justice of the Peace for Kingston.[13] Wyatt awarded Joe the sum of one guinea in damages.

Turn just a few pages in the Deposition Book and we find Thomas Woods was back before the Justice again. This time he was the plaintive, explaining that earlier that day he had been cutting Ling on Byfleet Common when he was approached by three other broom-makers, John Southey, Thomas Young and Thomas Hummick, all from Chertsey. Forcibly they stole eight bundles of his Ling, with Hummick threatening that if Woods resisted "*he would chop him down with a hook which he had in his hand.*"

People like broom-makers living off the heathland economy, after the Enclosures, could have the very poorest of livings; life was tough and so were the people. They became known as 'heathers', pronounced 'heethers'. Many a 'Heather Cottage' beside the heathlands today was originally a 'heether' cottage. They had a reputation for uncouth language and violent behaviour, which led to 'heether' being used as an insult - I remember my father in the

Ling besom back in use:
Oakhurst Cottage, Hambledon,
Surrey, in care of the National
Trust, furnished as per c. 1850

mid 1950s being felled with a single blow from someone whom he had just abused in this way. At the same period 'Heather' was a local surname and was still pronounced 'heether' although that has died out now in favour of the normal 'heather'. Confusion and prejudice arose also with the arrival of doorstep salespeople, who were liable to be called gypsies. Often they weren't. Gypsies were mobile whereas heathers stayed put. Both social groups could be making and selling brooms.

Such language goes back to Saxon times. Indeed, it links with Roman Britain. The first Roman Christian communities were in urban centres, from where they could look over the town walls and see the little communities of the countryside, where the evangelists had yet to penetrate. Here the rural people, known as *pagani*, still followed their separate religions and gave us the notion of *pagan*. The Saxons arrived with much the same idea and that has persisted into modern German with *der Heide* for heather and *die Heiden* for pagan, from which we get 'heathen'.

The Saxons called brooms 'besoms', pronounced bezom or bizom in the south and beezom in the north. They also had the word 'brom' from which we get 'broom' but how they differentiated between them I have never heard. Possibly a broom was the softer, more flexible version made from the shrub they called Broom (*Cytisus scoparius*) while the coarser versions, made from Ling and Birch, were besoms. The softer were almost certainly used by the medieval textile industry for sweeping shearings off the stretched cloth, without snagging up the nap, whereas besom came down through the Middle Ages with meanings associated with coarse, vigorous, abrasive sweeping. The Oxford English Dictionary exemplifies with the grand "*Swepe thy soul clene wyth the besome of the drede of God.*"

The makers of the brooms, in modern times, have regional names. In Surrey, those of the Wey valley, From Chertsey in the north to the Sussex/Hants border in the south, were 'squarers', that became 'squires'. To the west of this region is the Blackwater Valley where they were known as 'bashers' or 'dashers'. The two regions were linked by heathlands and so there were squires on the east side and dashers on the west side. The squires in the south, in The Devil's Punch Bowl, featured in a Victorian novel, *The Broom-Squire*, by S. Baring Gould. It's a frustrating source of evidence for despite evoking the scenes and the life-style so vividly it does it all without a paragraph of description. One of the cottages featured is now the Youth Hostel. Most of the others lie in ruins in the adjacent undergrowth.

Nightjar, which was going into sharp decline until the restoration of the heathlands, since when it has increased dramatically on many sites.
Drawn from a photograph taken by Peter Haines

GRAZING

IN THE OLD MANORIAL DAYS

When the Normans arrived they found that most of England was divided already into administrative units and that these were functioning in a highly successful way; late-Saxon culture was the most advanced in northern Europe. Upon this the Normans imposed their feudal manorial system that flourished until the coming of the Black Death in 1348, after which more changes came with the Peasants Revolt in 1381. The agricultural emphasis shifted heavily onto sheep farming for England's famous woollen industry. The southern heathlands supported vast numbers of sheep. There were so many thousands of them it is almost impossible to imagine it today.

The early medieval manors aimed to be as self-supporting as possible. Their lands were demarcated into areas for woodlands and coppices, pastures and arable lands, with some arable set aside each year to lie fallow so that soil fertility could recover. There was also the 'waste'. That word has changed its meaning, to that of 'unusable' but originally it meant 'unploughed'. Normally that meant *never* ploughed. It was far from unusable. It was at times the most valuable of the manorial lands.

The foremost problems for the medieval communities were feeding themselves and their livestock through the long winter months. In terms of the latter, when the grass stopped growing and there was no grazing, all they had to rely on was hay. There was rarely enough of that, even after culling some of the livestock in November, and of course it depended upon the success of last season's hay crop. Wet weather at haymaking time was a savage blow and recurrent wet summers in the later Middle Ages ensured famines every few years for people and animals alike. The importance of hay was known starkly.

Consequently, it was about mid-April when minds turned to the approaching season. It was imperative to safeguard as much grassland as possible, whether in designated pastures or alongside trackways, field edges or wherever. That meant stopping the livestock from eating it, so that the grasses and wild flowers among them could shoot up to flower. Then there would be the greatest bulk *and* it would be at its most nutritious, full of nitrogen compounds from which to make proteins plus sugars and starches from which to get energy. There were also such compounds as coumarins that would give the hay an appetising smell and flavour, while other herbs contained digestive stimulants etc. The manorial courts decided upon a day when the livestock must be removed from the pastures to allow this promise to be fulfilled. Two problems arose. One was space. Several thousand sheep take up a lot of room! Secondly, wherever they were put they needed food. Both problems were solved readily where manors had heathlands as part of their 'waste' - plenty of room *and* the animals could eat it. That's where the livestock were moved and fed upon the Ling and associated plants. Interestingly, in places where grazing practices have persisted, such as West Wales, the peak time for using heathland is in this May-June period. Also, current grazing experiments are revealing that it is at this back end of winter through spring that the livestock are keenest to eat Ling.

It appears to have been such a commonplace practice that it did not get written down very often. Thus an historical survey of one small heath found only three references in the documentary history of that site, from which the archaeologist concluded that the village grazed its heath rarely. Think again. The study was of the *heathland* but should have included an overview of the *whole* manor. The village and its lands were very small, in a typical South East England way so they had no choice but to maximise all their resources. The population appears to be have been stable, following the same fluctuations as their neighbouring ones, and they profited to the extent of maintaining a good, decent parish church that still stands. However, their pasturelands were limited. They could only have succeeded in producing enough hay if they diverted grazing on to their heathland. It's a story that can be repeated hundreds of times for all the similar communities. The pastures of this particular village were down along the river and it is known that they suffered floods. The heathlands were their insurance policy against such times, for they could move their livestock to the higher ground, where there was both room and food. Similarly, when the lowlands were heavily frosted and couldn't be grazed, the livestock could be moved to the heathland on higher ground. It was above the frost pocket and more exposed to winds that kept the frost off. Again, when blizzards dumped deep snow in the river valley the winds often scoured the high ground. The heathland was not wasted; it was an invaluable insurance against adversity.

GRAZING INTO MODERN TIMES

Livestock through the Middle Ages changed little. Although the worst individuals were culled at Martinmass there was little scope for improvement when the lord of the manor and the bishop had the right to claim the best and second best beasts as 'death duties' when the head of a family died. Records show this right was not exercised fully; it was in everybody's interest to keep the communities going. When that system changed there was scope for livestock improvement. The emphasis on sheep-rearing declined as the wool industry moved northwards, off the southern heathlands. There were still thousands of sheep but cattle were becoming more numerous;

consumption of cows' milk overtook sheep milk in the mid 16th century. Any tour through Britain in the 17th and 18th centuries, would have revealed endless variation in the cattle and other livestock. Today's monotonous repetition of large black and white cows did not exist, nor did the division into the recognised breeds of say fifty years ago. Instead, cattle were small and closely inbred, creating regional but variable types. Then astute stockmen singled

Longhorns today

out the best and started breeding them selectively,[14] until ultimately Britain had distinct breeds, with names reflecting their regional origins: the Ayrshires, Guernseys, Jerseys, Herefords, etc. Some breeds became numerous but still local, such as the Kerry, Dexter and Sussex. All were primarily dual-purpose breeds - for beef and milk. The expansion of urban communities through industrialisation would create markets that would change that, as specialism became viable. Thus the Shorthorns became either Beef Shorthorns or Dairy Shorthorns. That of course is 'mainstream' agriculture.

Many people had no choice but to continue the traditional ways and benefited from two qualities in their cattle, which were otherwise being abandoned. One was hardiness. The 18th century saw the rise of farmyards surrounded by specialised buildings, including stalls, in which the cattle could be housed comfortably during bad weather. The second great virtue is often described as 'thriftiness'. The cattle could thrive on poor pastures, including heathlands, and were adept at finding any wholesome plants among the coarse grasses and shrubs. Their counterparts in mainstream agriculture were being pampered in fields sown with special mixtures of nutritious grasses and clover and there was an increasing provision of winter feed other than hay, starting with turnips and followed by other root crops, maize and silage. Growing these on 'mixed' farms required space. Poorer farmers did not have the land. Many still practised Commoners' Rights to find enough grazing at all. By the 1970s the exercising of Commoners Rights on the heathlands was restricted to just a few places. Elsewhere, in the absence of grazing, trees such as Birch, Pine and Oak were colonising the heathlands and shading out the specialised flora of Ling and Furze. The appearance of heathlands was changing dramatically.

Leaf litter from the broad-leaved trees can change the nature of the soil (from podsol to brown earth) and thereby make it hostile to Ling and other heathland plants. By this time, however, the decline of the working countryside in general was giving rise to concerns and 'conservation' became a prime issue. On the heathlands, countryside wardens led teams of volunteers at the backbreaking task of uprooting the invading tree seedlings but that needed doing year after year and inevitably enthusiasm waned. Another word crept into popularity - 'sustainable'. It was realised that just as heathlands had been maintained by grazing for thousands of years so the reintroduction of livestock on to the heathlands could be a sustainable conservation measure. It would not be possible on every site and nor would it be the sole solution but it did have potential. However, when modern cattle were tried they did not thrive. The old traits of thriftiness and hardiness had been bred out of them. People turned to the old breeds, since some, but not all, still survived.

Some were very old indeed, descended from the wild cattle of prehistory, such as the white Park Cattle. They are a bit wild though so attention turned to the docile British Whites that some people think have been here 4,000 years (Illus. title page). So valued was this stock that it was this breed, and only this breed, that the Government exported to the United States in 1940 as a safeguard in case Britain be invaded during the war. British Whites excelled in

America, in both the cold and the heat, and earned fulsome praise, leading ultimately to the founding of the British White Cattle Association of America in 1987. They are beautiful animals: short-coated, white, with black knees, ears, eyes and noses. Their black eyes have proved resistant to eye cancer while the cows' teats, which are also black, are resistant to sunburn. Bulls are docile and very efficient at converting food into meat, with a low back-fat measurement. Cows breed every year, calve without problems and then become excellent mothers, producing ample quantities of rich milk (the butterfat, nearly 4%, is good for soft cheese). The praise heaped on them would make even a white cow blush. Needless to say, British Whites are now widespread in the world, from Britain to America and Australia. Originally they were developed in mid-Lancashire and Cheshire and later became popular in East Anglia, before becoming more widely known. Out on the heathlands their virtues lie in their thriftiness with poor vegetation and have been used by the Surrey Heathland Project. Their docility is a great advantage where there is public access and the Surrey Project even had one in Woking town centre for a day to promote the project. They are tough but not as hardy as the Scottish Highland or the Galloway.

When conservationists were looking for something tough they thought of the Scottish Highland Cattle. Their long shaggy coats would be more than enough protection through southern heathland winters and they flourish on Ling. They are thought to contain genes of the ancient Celtic cattle but cattle raids over the English border brought back to Scotland a whole mixture of other genes. Nevertheless they remain very distinctive with their long, thick, coats and wide-spreading upturned horns, which all help to endear them to the public. That's important because using livestock requires the erection of fencing to separate animals from vehicles but the very mention of fencing even part of a heathland can be anathema to some people. So the attractiveness of Highland cattle is important and these animals are reassuringly docile, even the bulls. It's the cows that can be a bit wild at calving time but they need not be on the heathlands at that time. They only produce enough milk to feed the calf and then only for a short time, so they do not require a lot of man-hours in that regard. They do return fine beef though. The National Trust, among others, have used them to graze such properties as the Devil's Punch Bowl and Witley Common, in Surrey

A very different beast is the Longhorn, with amazing sweeping horns. They were so widely distributed in Britain that they have been described as the 'national' breed. Originally they came from the Craven district of Yorkshire, whence they spread over the Midlands and ultimately into most English counties, to become the most popular breed in the 18th century. This was one of the prime breeds used by Robert Bakewell in his selective breeding programme, as there was considerable variation around the country from which to choose. He concentrated on beef production since they produced good meat on lean carcasses (but even the fat was good for tallow). They were a bit slow at maturing though. The cows produced more than adequate supplies of milk, high in butterfat but with only small fat globules, which were good for cheese making. When other breeds, especially the shorthorn, came to the fore the Longhorns did not die out since they were needed still for their tradition role as draught animals - ox teams persisted in use until into the 20th century. They had performed that service for hundreds and hundreds of years; the white stripe down the back and right round to run up the stomach is taken as an indicator of very ancient lineage. Only two other breeds in the British Isles retain this white 'eelstripe' or 'finching', namely the Gloucester of Double Gloucester Cheese fame and the Irish Moyled. Thus Longhorns were targeted for trials in the modern heathland conservation movement, in Berkshire for example, where all their old qualities are so desirable. Despite their size and appearance they are remarkable docile. The bulls even allow stockmen into the group. Longhorns, on the whole, respond amazingly well to quiet, decent handling.

Longhorn

Cattle have dominated this discussion so far, but numerically speaking the most important livestock on the Heathlands have always been sheep. Even in late times, such as late 19th century. Suffolk, the old practices persisted still, of grazing the heaths during the day before moving the flocks onto the arable by night, to dung the land. It was with sheep that the first conservation measures began, in 1972, when the Nature Conservancy Counsel introduced them onto the chalk grassland of the National Nature Reserve at Aston Rowant in Buckinghamshire. Then in 1986 sheep were introduced onto the lowland heathland of Skipwith Common Nature Reserve, by the Yorkshire Wildlife Trust. It is the fact that sheep feed entirely differently from cattle that can be exploited by conservationists. Both types of animal have teeth in one jaw only and so there is a problem over severing the mouthful. Cattle wrap their tongues around the herbage and drag it across their teeth to cut it and therefore cannot cope with short fodder. Their limit is some 5-6cm. Sheep clamp the fodder against their teeth and give a little tug to sever it. In this way they can crop stuff down to just 3 cms. Ponies have teeth in both jaws and scissor stuff down to 2cm. Not only can this be exploited towards the desired aims of the management plan but the different animals have different preferences in fodder. Cattle are not all that keen on Ling if they have a choice and so this selectivity can be used to reduce competitive plants in favour of the Ling. Sheep enjoy Ling. They can be used to reduce its height to create specific habitats for certain wildlife species. In fact sheep are much more selective about what they eat than are cattle, and even spit out their mistakes! They don't like dead material either whereas cattle deliberately take a proportion of woody material into their daily diet. A further important factor is that sheep are light and dainty, and may not damage the landscape so traumatically as heavy hoofed cattle and ponies. Heavy hooves crush emerging Bracken croziers and retard this unwelcome fern, whereas sheep step daintily over them.

In terms of sheep breeds, there were several ancient ones from which to choose. The public would have enjoyed the Soay sheep, as they are so attractive, but when they were tried it was found that when disturbed by visitors and their dogs they scattered in all directions and were nearly impossible to round up. Attention then turned to the black Hebrideans with their curly horns. The Hebrideans are very ancient, having been brought to the Scottish islands from Scandinavia hundreds of years ago. They are very hardy in exposed conditions and very thrifty feeders. They can make short work of Purple Moor Grass and if not managed carefully can destroy it within two years. They chomp the leaf right down and the plant only needs to lose a third of its foliage to suffer retardation. Then they carry on and destroy the tussocks themselves. This is an important consideration where the grass cover is expanding at the expense of the Ling and works well because the Hebridean prefers to eat the grass rather than the Ling. The Swaledale sheep, on the other hand, prefer Ling to the grass.

A third significant option is to turn to ancient breeds of pony, such as the Exmoor and the Dartmoor, which are thought to have derived from pre-historic herds. The Exmoor ponies have fossils going back 100,000 years and remain one of the hardiest of Britain's nine native breeds of pony. They have a very thick undercoat to trap the body heat and so efficient is this that warmth does not escape through to melt snow on the overcoat of the pony's back. The overcoat is of long guard hairs, waterproofed with oil that draw together with the rain to form triangles that shed the water from the downward points. The eyes are set under a fleshy ridge (toad-eye) which shelters them from driving rain and biting winds. They drop their heads and turn away from the wind so that the body protects them, and their rear ends are in turn protected by the thick tail. They survive whatever the weather throws at them. The foal (never twins) is born early, in April or early May, so it has a chance to mature sufficiently to withstand its first winter.

The New Forest Ponies were in that locality long before William the Conqueror designated it a hunting reserve. Their existence was recorded by the Saxons in the early 11th century and in the next century they became the property of the local people, so establishing their place in the commoners' grazing rights. Since the 13th century there has been selective culling of weak and unworthy ponies so the breed has remained strong. Over the last 250 years, in common with the Dartmoors and other breeds, there has been a lot of hybridizing to get 'improvements'. Nevertheless, the ancient genes survive. The foals are born a little later than the Exmoors, in May and June, and are nurtured by their mothers through the summer. They are not such good breeders as the Exmoors and neither are they quite so long-lived. The foals, being born later, do not have so long to mature before their first winter but in the New Forest the herds can shelter form the worst of the weather in the wooded areas. Here they change their diet from heathland plants to such favourites as the woodland Holly and Brambles. They take a lot of the woody material and in any case they have to eat twice as much as cattle, seeing as they are not ruminants that can chew the cud to extract maximum nutrition.

Goats have a long history on the heathlands too but there is far less documentation for goat husbandry than for other livestock. Modern trials have found that goats enjoy eating Scots Pines whereas nothing else likes its food flavoured with turpentine. This seems to be reflected in the documents:- the Scots Pines disappear from the records from mid Saxon times right through to the 17th century. That is the very period when kid meat was held in high esteem. When it fell from favour and there was less goat herding on the heathlands, so the pines were able to regenerate freely again. The foregoing is not proven fact, yet. Goats are not the wonder solution to controlling pines today, for although they eat pines from Monday to Friday, come the weekends they eat visitors' handbags. Visitors' dogs also torment them. Consequently, their use in conservation is restricted to private heathlands. For example, they are used most effectively on the Ministry of Defence lands at Ash Ranges in Surrey.

Although not universally important today, other livestock, such as pigs and poultry, have been out on the heathlands in the past. Commoners' rights for both exist still on the Pembrokeshire heathlands. Exotics have been tried too from Przewalski horses in Hampshire to water buffalo in Berkshire. An odd little use of Ling is the Irish 'spancel' - a twisted cord of stems used to tether the leg of a hen to stop it wandering off.

BURNING

The livestock of the heathlands were introduced in the previous sections together with what we are learning today about their management. Much of the traditional knowledge has been lost and having to be rediscovered. That includes techniques for stimulating Ling and associated plants into producing a good browse of new growth in the spring. Up on the northern moors there is the long tradition of 'swaling' - of burning off the old, woody and dead material. Whether the southern heathlands were fired on a regular basis in the past is a vexed question. There are some who believe firmly that it was, since the commoners of the New Forest do it today and have memories of this 'tradition' going back several generations. Beware; the Victorians promoted heavily all manner of activities as 'traditional' when they were nothing of the sort. Records from before 1800 need to be sought. These are rare but as there is always a shortage of documentation for ordinary, every day working life this paucity is not entirely surprising. However, as this would be a special event, organised originally through the memorial courts, there ought to be more references, especially if the fires got out of control. Even when agricultural 'improvement' was highly fashionable, in the 17th century, the textbooks are not full of instructions and warnings. That said, the practice in the New Forest should not be disregarded.

An important question is whether people *needed* to burn. Today, firing is much concerned with getting rid of the build-up of dead litter that is retarding the natural regeneration of Ling, grasses and other fodder plants. It also kills off tree seedlings that would shade out the desirables and it creates bare ground in which Ling seeds germinate. It is difficult to imagine these being problems on the *smaller* heathlands in the past. By *smaller* think not of the overall extent on the ground but in terms of the size of portion of that expanse that was held by each of the surrounding manors. They not only needed it for grazing but the Ling and other plants were put to a considerable variety of other uses. In total these would have put pressure upon the growing areas, probably to the extent of obviating the problems of today's commoners. Let's look briefly at four of the main problems. Firstly, tree seedlings would have been grazed off;

even the little leaves of the Birches are massive compared to those of Ling. Oak leaves are even bigger. Where trees were wanted, such as Birch for coppicing to grow besom material, they would need protecting from livestock. Secondly, Furze shoots are spineless and make good fodder; it was actually grown as a fodder crop, even to the extent of seeding it with corn ready for when the livestock were turned onto the stubble after the harvest. If protected from grazing it was coppiced on an eighteen-month cycle, for fuel, so there was little chance of it maturing into big bushes, except where areas were set aside for that purpose. There is evidence that they were. Thirdly, there is the problem of the spread of Bracken and build-up of its dead litter. That should not have happened. Up to three demands per year could be made by a manor on its growing Bracken, to satisfy different needs, plus the removal of any remaining litter for bedding. If they did that consistently for over four years they would have killed the bracken so restraint was exercised. Fourthly, there is the problem of the Ling ageing and losing vigour. It takes some fifteen years to reach maximum potential and another fifteen in decline, unless it is cut or burnt to rejuvenate it. Much of it was cut, for thatching and broom-making materials. In addition to the above there is a list of minor uses. With all this going on, in say 1600, would there really have been a need to burn it off and start again? The manor would lose an area out of production while it was regenerating - did they have enough heathland to afford that?

Obviously a crucial question is whether the manors really did crop the heathlands so heavily. There is plenty of documentation relating to such harvests but not necessarily telling in detail the activities of a given manor in a given year, let alone a succession of years. Accounts relate normally to trade and therefore do not include material taken for the community's personal domestic needs. The best evidence gets overlooked and that is the wildlife. Ecologists record an amazing variety of wildlife dependent upon heathlands and many species have very specific requirements, from bare ground right up through the varying heights of Ling at different stages. This reflects a heathland being a mosaic of micro-habitats - and that is exactly what would have resulted from harvesting in the past. If we could go back, to say 1600 again, and view a community's heathland we would find two main divisions of usage. Firstly there was the area reserved for grazing and turf cutting. Secondly there was the area safeguarded from grazing and cutting to enable the Ling to reach maturity, to be cut on rotation for thatching and broom-making. These worked ideally on a five to seven year cycle, depending upon the prevailing growing conditions. Thus this area of the heathland would exhibit five to seven different micro-habitats, reflecting the previous succession of harvests. Bearing in mind that most species of fauna take an incredibly long time to adapt to environmental change, this testifies to the fact that in the past, these micro-habitats must have been in widespread and persistent existence. There is such a range of species demanding Ling at a particular height/stage that it is difficult to believe these needs could have been met without the intensive cropping described. To save declining species the early conservators restored larger areas of Ling but that still failed to halt the decline. When they tried cutting swathes to ensure areas all at the same stage the blue butterflies etc. flourished. They don't like it intermingled; they want it en-mass, just as it must have been for centuries in the past. Now you can see such mown swathes, especially for the butterflies etc. on many heathlands, such as the Iping and Stedham Commons in West Sussex and Frensham Common in Surrey.

That does not mean that such micros-habitats were *never* created by fire. The species demanding bare ground are interesting. Did they evolve this preference from the rectangles cut out by turf cutting or are they testifying to the use of fire? Seeing as adaptation is so slow we can be sure that areas of bare ground were always available and that implies turf-cutting, unless burning was practised annually. An annual burning is doubted, following studies of its impact upon the soil chemistry. Burning the heathland changes its chemistry. About 95% of the nitrogen is lost but a presence is essential for plant regeneration. In the past, nitrogen-fixing plants such as Furze and Broom, may have been all-important for replenishing it. Today, it gets rained down in air pollution, in concentrations so high that they cause concern. Other essential nutrients that will be lost include calcium, magnesium, potassium and sodium. These are replenished within a few years by natural means. It is the loss of phosphorus that is more telling. That takes about twenty years to be replaced. Such chemical changes affect the whole biodiversity of the affected heathland. There is the additional factor that fire destroys the litter-layer, which itself plays a crucial part. When these chemical changes and the time intervals needed for their replenishment (particularly phosphorus) are put with the maturation cycle of the Ling, the conclusion is that if burning was practised at all, then it is most likely to have been on a twenty year cycle.

One micro-habitat that might have been burnt more regularly is that where Purple Moor Grass has colonised. This is a really tough grass, with two special characteristics. It is Britain's only deciduous grass so that shedding spent foliage is not an ongoing process but happens in bulk at the end of autumn. That leaves nothing with which to start growth the next year and so its other speciality is storing food. That happens at the bases of the stems causing swellings that eventually become sizeable tussocks. It could well be that these were burnt off to stimulate re-growth and make it more accessible. However, there was a demand for this leaf-litter, resulting in it being stripped from the land, for animal bedding and making up palliasses. The latter was one product of the heathlands that could be traded readily in towns. Even where the litter has been stripped off there would still have been a lot of dead stems etc protruding from the tussocks, plus dead matter in the tussocks themselves, which was maybe burnt off to encourage grazers to go straight in for the fresh blades in the spring.

In contrast, one plant testifies to a heathland not having been fired extensively for decades and that is the Juniper. Saplings do not withstand burning. During the twentieth century it has become extinct on many of the heathlands where it grew previously, as for example in West Surrey where massive spreading mature specimens were commented upon in 1904. They are a reminder that manors and private landowners managed the lands to serve their individual needs and priorities. When one might have used fire its neighbour might not. It is perhaps worth pointing out that a record of a fire does not testify to regular agricultural practice; there have always been lightening strikes, accidental fires and acts of malicious spite.

LING AND BEES

"This little poore creature the Bee, doth not onely with her laboure yeeld unto us her delicate and most healthy Hony, but also with the good example of her paineful dilligence and travail, encourageth man to labour and take paines according to his calling." (Barnaby Goodge, 1577)

Honey from heather is a product that is still well known today; thick and flavoursome with little air bubbles in it. There is another product though, that was once valued even more highly, and that was beeswax. *Calluna* in bloom provides a rich source of nectar. It is secreted from eight little swellings between the stamens, down in the base of the flower. Only a tiny amount is available in the flower at any one time, since the individual bells are so small but there may be several hundred of these on a long flowering shoot and dozens of those on a flourishing plant. No wonder the Ling is so attractive to bees. Once the nectar is converted into honey the bees have to produce all the wax for the comb cells and their lids. Beekeepers have valued the heathlands for thousands of years. Indeed the first beekeepers were the Bronze Age peoples who developed the heathlands. They wanted the wax for casting their metal tool heads. Much of the honey was left aside and fermented into mead, which is believed to be man's first alcoholic drink.

Honeybees would not have been commonplace on the earliest heathlands because there was no shelter or breeding holes or continuous supplies of food. It wasn't until the climate had warmed sufficiently after the last Ice Age to support a range of nectar-bearing flowers throughout the summer months that bees would have been able to expand their range into this corner of Europe; there was still no English Channel. Even when Ling was the dominant plant for many square miles there would only have been food for the bees for a few weeks each year. Therefore they would have been found round the fringes where better soils supported a wider range of plants. Similarly, it was here that they could find shelter and nesting-holes in ageing trees.

Skeps on their stools under their rye straw roofs. Example can still be seen in the 19th Century artwork of Birket Foster

Prehistoric man learned to seek out and raid the nests. Then he aimed for better control over the bees by imitating natural nest sites, with hollow logs, before weaving willow into a basin and thereby inventing the first bee skep. He had to learn to plaster it over with clay or dung to prevent draughts and rain entering through the chinks in the weaving. Bees are fussy about such niceties. Pieces of stick were wedged across the interior from which the bees could hang their combs. In due course weaving was replaced by coiling. Straw or grass was twisted into ropes and bound with the bark of honeysuckle, bramble or willow, and coiled round to make the dome. This avoided draughty little chinks but still needed plastering to keep out the rain, unless they were given a sheltering roof. By the 15th century special alcoves or 'boles' were built into house and garden walls in which to stand the skeps for protection. Remarkably this prehistoric skep continued in common usage until the 19th century. Cottagers who had to keep their skeps out in the open provided them with thatched shelters, made ideally with rye straw (as it was so long and cheap). By the 19th century William Cobbett instructed that these should be replaced every three or four months but this was obviously an ideal rather than a necessity, for those shown in some old paintings look decidedly decrepit! The 19th century Russian landscape painter, Ivan Shiskin, depicted what look like tall narrow wooden boxes but a pencil study[15] makes it quite clear that these are hollowed-out tree trunks with rough half-log lids/roofs. Does any reader know how long such trunks were in use in Britain before being superseded by skeps?

The trouble with skeps was that they did not utilise the available space efficiently and they precluded access for management purposes. They would be better if made as rectangular boxes with moveable sections. The bees defeated early attempts at this by cementing the moveable sections to the shell. Part of their natural behaviour is to collect resinous substances from plant buds and use it as a cement (called propolis or 'bee glue') to make their nest hole secure and free from draughts. Thus they sabotaged moveable parts in the same way. It wasn't until 1851 that this problem was overcome, by Rev. Lorenzo Lorraine Langstroth, an amateur beekeeper in Pennsylvania. He invented the 'bee space' which was a quarter inch gap between the combs that was found to be wide enough to allow bees through but too wide for them to cement with propolis. Other apiarists developed the idea further into the modern hives of today. These designs meant bees no longer had to be killed at harvest time as had been the case previously.

Killing was necessary to get at the contents of the skep and became a matter of standing the skep over a shallow pit in which sulphur was added to burning material. The fumes choked the skep and the bees fell out and died. Harvesting began at Michaelmas (29th September) when the heaviest skeps were destroyed for their load of honey and wax. The middle-weight skeps were kept, in which the bees overwintered. The lightest skeps were also destroyed since they did not contain enough food reserves to feed the bees right through the winter. The contents of comb, wax and honey were ripped out and crushed altogether in a long linen sock or 'poke' through which the honey could be strained. That sounds so straightforward in the textbooks but how was it done? Was the poke hung up and crushed by hand so that the honey ran down into a container below? Was it laid in the bacon-salting trough, on the ground, for the children to trample? Does any reader know?

By the 17th century public opinion was turning against killing the bees. They were considered one of God's very special creations and were practically sacred. The alternative to killing was to invert the full skep and place an empty one over it to make a sphere and then to rattle the bottom skep until the bees had fled into the upper one. This was not always successful! The new Langstroth hive was built in storeys that meant extra levels or 'supers' could be built above the summer hive for the bees to move into and be separated off from their earlier combs below. This increase in space had the added advantage of deterring the bees from swarming. Under improved management, harvesting was started at the end of July and lasted until the middle of September. The bees were left alone, theoretically, from 1st November until 1st April.

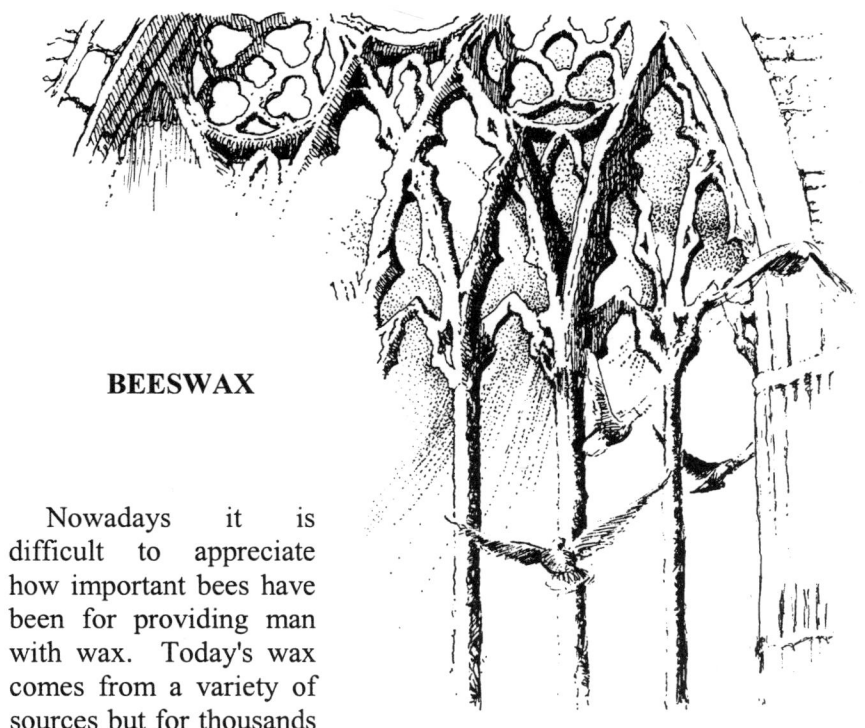

BEESWAX

Nowadays it is difficult to appreciate how important bees have been for providing man with wax. Today's wax comes from a variety of sources but for thousands of years honeybees were the prime or only source. It had a wide range of uses from candles to polish, from the basis of ointment to being a lubricant and waterproofer. It is secreted between scale-like plates on the underside of the abdomen of the worker bee and is used to build and repair the honeycomb and to cap the cells once they are full of honey. It is the worker bees that are responsible for these tasks, through a particular stage in their life cycles, starting when they are 10-16 days old, until superseded by the duty of receiving the nectar and pollen being brought back by the foraging workers. In due course they will become foragers themselves.

Although many cultures, such as the Greek and Roman, held bees sacred, it was the coming of Christianity to Britain that created an immense demand for beeswax, for making the church candles. The pre-Reformation Church in England used more lights than anywhere else in Christendom, 'owing probably to the greater gloom of our climate'. The Church viewed bees as a model of chastity and so candles came to symbolise Christ born of the Virgin. A medieval

Welsh document stated boldly that *'the origin of bees is from Paradise....therefore the Mass cannot be said without the wax'*, and this belief is reflected by the Catholic Church in the edict that only candles made from 100% beeswax could be burned for mass service. In the great churches that could mean fifty or more candles at the High Altar. Then there were more at the side altars, at the altar of the Lady Chapel, and at the altars in the chantry chapels and guild chapels. All of these could be celebrating separate mass services at the same time, striving to remain sufficiently synchronised for their Elevation of the Host to be in unison. The demand for beeswax candles was immense and the church couldn't scrape up the run-off from previous days and reuse it. That wax was described as 'yellow wax' and was disallowed. It was not wasted but used up for lighting the painted and carved images, including the great rood or crucifix, because it did not produce so much destructive blackening smoke as did tallow. For general lighting they used tallow (animal fat), which was far cheaper. The candles for lesser services, such as mattins, did not have to be of pure beeswax.

Thus medieval churches on great feast days were glorious with light. It must have been stunning to those who came from dark hovels where even a humble rush-light was a luxury. It must have been horrific to little children looking up at a dead man nailed on a cross with the glass inlays in his eyes glittering in the candlelight. Even little country churches, like Spelsbury in Oxfordshire had many altars and lights, which were recorded in the churchwardens' accounts. These survive from 1525-39. The fullest list, of 1531, gives the light, its cost and the day that cost was to be met. The administration required two wardens for each light. Indeed the number of wardens with special duties, plus the general wardens, involved some thirty men of the village. It's only a tiny place even today. At least the burden of the costs was spread throughout the year. Multiply this impression through the thousands of medieval parish churches and we begin to glimpse aspects of medieval life which otherwise go unnoted. The list, which may not be complete, impresses upon us the extent of the demand and its importance in the parishioners' year:-

Trinity light - Candlemas Day - 22s 8d
Our Lady's Light - Annunciation - 4s
Hersse Light - any date before Allhallowtide - 16s 10d
St. Nicholas's Light - 16s 2d
St. George's Light - St. Matthias Day - 22s 10d
St. Clement's Light - St. Clement's Eve - 5s 7d
St. Katherine's Light - St. Thomas of Canterbury - 8s 4d plus
three and a half strikes of barley [strike - usually one bushel but could be half]
St. Erasmus's Light - St. Stephen's Day - 4s 8d plus a sheep worth 20d and two bushels of barley
St. Christopher's Light - New Year's Eve - 4s 4d and two bushels barley
St. Anthony's Light - Shrove Monday - 14s
St. Michael's Light - St. Michael's Day - 2s and four bushels barley
St. Andrew's Light

The cost of wax was the greatest of all charges met by the English Catholic Church and so to get enough the parishioners were taxed in wax as part of their tithes or they paid rents in wax. It was only the combined efforts of all the parishioners' small skeps that kept the churches lighted. People bequeathed money to their church specifically for lights, often specifying the weight of the candle they had in mind; or else they bequeathed a field from which the sale of the crops was intended to fund lights. The church at Cowfold, Sussex, owned nine oxen and four cows which they farmed out to raise funds for church lighting - two of the cows sustained four tapers in honour of St. Katherine while the other two funded a light for St. Anthony and for Our Lady. At Arlington, Sussex, the church farmed twenty-eight cows for two pounds of wax each but even those fifty six pounds of wax a year wouldn't have gone very far.[16]

The great size of some of the candles is quite overwhelming today. The Paschal candle, lit during a special ceremony from the newly blessed fire on Easter morning and remaining in the sanctuary till Ascension Day, weighted two hundred pounds or more, which has been calculated to be a year's work for 20,000 bees. The great font candle was lit during another solemn ceremony at the blessing of the font on the eve of Easter and Whitsun and was lit at all subsequent baptisms, so that must have been quite a size. Lighting in monastic churches was very important because services took place at intervals through the night. Tallow was permitted for general use but not for services at the High Altar. That demanded beeswax again but there might be only one candle. It was a different matter if the monastery housed the tombs of important nobles or royalty requiring votive lights at all times. Westminster Abbey, for example, had to find 1,434 pounds of beeswax per year once it had to provide votive lights at the tombs of Richard II, Henry III, V and VI and Queen Eleanor. Special processions must have caused quite a problem - the funeral of Henry V, for example, had sixty bearers of beeswax torches and that lot weighed a total 870 pounds - or about the weight of five men!

The lights were made by monks and other monastery workers where such were allowed. In the great secular houses (which used candles as clocks - six per day marked off in 20-minute intervals) it was the work of the servants. Despite all this effort demand could not be met and so chandlery became a specialised occupation by the 13th century. At that time they had become so well established as to be one of London's great trade guilds. There is mention then of their Hall which was in Gresham Street. It fell to the Great Fire of 1666 but has been rebuilt, several times. Today the Worshipful Company of Wax Chandlers ranks number twenty in the City's order of precedence. They have as their grace:-

> For thy creature the bee,
> The wax and the honey,
> We thank thee, O Lord.

The late flowering of the Ling must have been a wonderful bonus in many areas as it extended the working season the bees. There was little else for the bees to work since many of the early autumn bee-plants we might think of today, such as the Michaelmas Daisies, were not introduced into this country until after the Reformation. By then the high demand for beeswax had fallen. The Reformation banned altar candles, banned chantry lights, banned wax effigies, and the monasteries were closed. It was the monasteries that developed bee-keeping. The responsibility fell ultimately to the cellarer who usually kept his skeps in the curia or outer court. It was he who would have initiated the procession bearing the skeps on planks, out towards the heathland, for an end of season bonus to a vital harvest.

LING HONEY

Honey was the nectar of the gods: sweeter than anything else in Britain for thousands of years; nutritious, healing, and one luxury the Church didn't frown upon - unless you got drunk upon the mead made from it.

Honey is made up largely of sugars (c.70-80%) plus minerals, amino acids and vitamins of the B-complex. Worker bees suck out the nectar from the eight little swellings below the stamens in the Ling flower and then in special parts of their stomachs they mix it with enzymes to form honey. This is regurgitated by the worker bees when they return to the nest and pass it over to a different grade of worker who packs it into the comb cells. A worker will visit some two million flowers to make a pound of honey and that requires some 25,000 trips back to the nest, at a speed of about 20 kph. At least Ling produces masses of flowers very close together and it *must* be from *Calluna* if the honey is to be traded as 'heather honey'. Nectar from *Erica* and *Daboecia* doesn't count in this context, even if collected with the *Calluna*; it has to be traded as 'flower honey'.

Thus to get 'heather honey' the apiarist needs to be able to place his hives in areas of Ling large enough to sustain the bees without them having to forage further afield, such as in the New Forest. In upland regions apiarists can take their hives to such a high altitude that there is only *Calluna* flowering and then a very pure honey can be obtained. This is probably the origin of the false notion that Ling only produces nectar if it is growing at altitudes in excess of 300m. What is true is that *Calluna* is very variable in nectar production. The flowering period is from July to September but nectar is released for only part of that time and even that is not predictable. Every three to five years it goes to the extreme and produces a glut of the stuff, rather like oak and beech having a 'mast' year. The trees probably fruited more regularly in the Middle Ages, or else it wouldn't have been possible to work the manorial system of pannage so perhaps the Ling was more consistent then too. The timing of rainfall seems to be one factor here. Despite this variability there is normally a reasonable flow most years and so people like those of the New Forest are able to market their famous honey.

Bee Skeps
Left: entrance from underneath.
Right: entrance from side at base

One of the problems of trying to work Ling is that it flowers late and thereby fails to synchronise with the life cycle of the bees. Encouraging them to carry on working it can leave the bees in a poor state to try and survive the winter but this was probably of little concern in the days when so many skeps were destroyed at the end of the season anyway. Today's apiarists show far greater concern over the well being of their bees. After all, they are very valuable, particularly for pollinating our crops. Now we have learned how to manage life in the hives to extend the forage season without doing harm.

Another problem with heather honey that it is thixotropic, which means it is a jelly rather than a liquid. That makes it difficult to extract from the comb cells. It has to be agitated, which makes it liquefy and run. Stop agitating it and the stuff sets again. The combs used to be removed and crushed inside straining cloths, under special presses, but modern technology has advanced beyond that now. It is not even essential to follow either practice since there is a demand for honey still in the comb, known as 'cut-comb honey'. For this, heather honey is ideal, simply because the jelly does *not* run out.

The insatiable demand for beeswax from the Roman Catholic Church through the Middle Ages ensured there were always copious supplies of honey. Sometimes the Church wanted both, as in this Surrey record of lands that included heaths:-

"William de Henley had held the manor of Henley, valued at £30 a year, exclusive of a quiterent, with other lands in Framelsworth [today's Frimley] *of the Abbot of Chertsey by the service of 22s 8d a year and twelve gallons of honey at Michaelmas."*[17]

Fortunately honey had no rivals at that time as a sweetener for although cane sugar was available from Norman times it was often twenty times more expensive. Herbal sweeteners were known and used, such as Angelica, *Angelica archangelica*, Sweet Cicely, *Myrrhis odorata* and Liquorice, *Glycyrrhiza glabra*.

Some of the honey was used as medicine, the value of which had been known since ancient times. The Roman soldiers had carried honey with them to use as a vulnerary for dressing wounds. This was valid because the bees put an enzyme into the honey, which has an antibacterial action that does not have adverse side effects upon the healthy tissue surrounding the wound. Neither does it dry up and harden round wounds, like most other dressings. No doubt the Romans were glad of it for sore feet. Since ancient times honey has been exploited for coughs, sore throats and other respiratory problems and remains an important demulcent and sweetener in British medicine, mostly in linctuses and cough mixtures. However, the *British Pharmacopoeia* warns, "*honey should not be given to infants because of the risk of causing infant botulism.*" This is due to honey having been identified as a carrier of the spores of the offending *Clostridium botulinum.*[18]

Allowing honey to ferment produces mead, which is claimed to be the world's oldest alcoholic drink. Adding fruit to the honey not only changed the flavour but was also a quicker way of adding yeast. The best fruits to choose were elderberries because they are the richest source of wild yeast, while also providing colour and flavour. In due course herbs and spices were added too. Thus by the time of the earliest sagas and myths, from the Irish to the Viking, we find references to the drinking of mead - usually prodigious drinking, with the inevitable results. The Norse poem *Hávamál* describes this so beautifully as "*the heron of oblivion hovers over the drinking bout.*" Even allowing for literary exaggeration, it is clear that the finest quality meads were of high social status. It was the drink of the gods and could hold special powers; thus in *Hávamál*, we read how the great god Odin contrived to steal the skaldic mead in order to get his poetic powers.[19] In the great hall of the slain, Valhalla, Odin provided a continuous supply of mead for the great feast each evening. It flowed from the udder of the goat Heidrun and was served up to the warriors in drinking horns carried to them by the Valkyries.[20] We can imagine the same high status among mankind, drinking mead to please their gods by imitation. It is clear from Egil's Saga that by the late 9th century Britain was exporting honey to the Vikings in Scandinavia, where there were severe penalties in law for making or selling 'false honey'.

By the early Middle Ages the Welsh had developed this as *meddyglyn* (combining *meddyg* meaning medicinal with *llyn* for liquor). Eventually the Welsh yielded this to the English as *metheglyn* (earliest Eng. ref. 1533) and it became very popular, especially the spiced version, which was much to the liking of Elizabeth I. A version using apples became known as *cyser* and a recipe using mulberries (high status) made *morat*. Alternatively, spices and unfermented honey could be added to wine for *clare, clary* and *claret* which were originally (before c.1600) yellowish or light red wines.

Mulberry

HEATHER ALE

Ling plays not only an important part in the making of mead but the flowering shoots can be made into ale. A very fine ale it is too, with the old recipes back in commercial production today.[21] It is a very old drink indeed; archaeologists working on the Scottish Isle of Rhum found a shard of a vessel in which the residue, when analysed, was found to be of a fermented drink made from Ling flowers, in c.2000 BCE. Types of 'heather ale', or *leann fraoich* in Gaelic, were widespread and famous by the time of the earliest written records of the North, whether relating to the Picts and other Scottish peoples or to Scandinavians. The Vikings would have spread their version south, into the Danelaw and beyond, where no doubt there was a local variety already.

There would have been many local variations, depending upon the choice and availability of the ingredients. The basics were malt, fresh water, yeast and sweetener, to which gruits or brewing herbs were added. In the north it was much more difficult to get barley for malting and it becomes an import, featuring regularly in the old laws of Norway. It was possible to make a heather ale without malt once Hops, *Humulus lupulus*, came into use, as per modern recipes, by boiling the flowering Ling tops in a little water for an hour, straining it and adding hops, ginger and golden syrup. Yeast is added after the mixture has been boiled and strained and cooled. After a few days' fermentation the ale is taken off, leaving the yeast deposit behind. In the days before golden syrup sweetening was provided by Angelica, *Angelica archangelica*. Note this recipe does not contain malt and could therefore be derived ultimately from very old practices. Supplies of malt would not have been such a major problem in England as it was for the Vikings in Norway. In the processing of the malt Ling was used too: a quotation in the Oxford English Dictionary under the entry for 'heather' informs us from 1633 that in the north, *'they dry their malt with ling, or heath...'* No doubt that gave it a distinctive flavour too.

It would have been with the additional herbs that local variation came to the fore. Such herbs were important not just to give variety to the flavour but to impart 'keeping' qualities. Judging by some Norwegian[22] plant names the Vikings arrived here with a working knowledge of 'beer grass' (*Filipendula ulmaria*). To the Saxons this was *'medewyrt'* and they used its antibiotic qualities in medicinal salves and held it in such esteem that it was included in their 'holy' salve.[23] Through the Middle Ages this became Meadsweet from its use in flavouring mead and then Meadow-sweet in the 16th century, by which name we still know it. It likes to grow in wet places but not as acidic as those on the heathlands so this is a herb that needed gathering from further afield. By today's standards we might find it imparted an odd taste, for the plant contains powerful antiseptics, which are so good they are in commercial use - crush young growth and the smell will bring to mind two well-known medicinal brands.

The Vikings had a name meaning 'beer king' for the three plants we know as Perforated St. John's Wort, *Hypericum perforatum*, Water Avens, *Geum rivale*, and Yarrow, *Achillea millefolium*. They gave the name 'beer-man' to Selfheal, *Prunella vularis* and also Yarrow again. All have a long history of usage for their antibiotic action except St. John's Wort, which is an anti-depressant but that must have added to the feeling of intoxication. English plant names relating to ale are few: primarily Alecost, *Tanacetum balsamita* and Alehoof, *Glechoma hederacea* but we too have used Yarrow, plus Nettles, *Urtica dioica*, Betony, *Stachys officinalis*, and Dandelion flowers, *Taraxacum officinale*. Although the bitter herbs, that provided natural preserving compounds, were replaced by Hops in the Middle Ages there was prejudice against them[24] and so other traditional herbs persisted in some places:

"About Shenston, as I was inform'd by the worthy Mr Frith of Thorns, they frequently used the Erica vulgaris, heath or ling, instead of hopps to preserve their beer, which, as he also told me, gave it no ill tast."

(Robert Plot; *Natural History of Staffordshire;* 1686)

St. John's Wort (Hypericum perforatum), known in parts of Norway as the 'Beer King'. Can be found in Britain in rough grassy places among brambles, etc. at the edge of areas of Ling. Drawn here on Esher Common, Surrey.

The Norse literature not only holds this ale and the mead in high esteem but highlights the strength of it. It has been calculated that their strong brew could possibly contain 10% alcohol. Even so, the references raise the possibility that the effects were increased by some of the brewing herbs, such as the popular Bog Myrtle or Sweet Gale (*Myrica gale*) that grows in wet heathland. Certainly it occurs in English ethnobotany in this context. In 1568 William Turner, the 'Father of English Botany' reported cheerily, "*It is tried by experience that it is good to be put in beer both by me and by divers others in Somerset.*" (*A New Herball*; part III). That was followed in John Gerard's herbal by the terse, "*fit to make a man quickly drunke*" and by 1791 William Lewis, in his *Experimental History of the Materia Medica*, reports its use "*as a substitute for hops for preserving malt liquors, which they render more inebriating and of consequence less salubrious.*" The shrub certainly contains a number of powerful compounds and these have been used in medicine - used warily since a little does good but too much is emetic or worse. Another herb from the wet heathlands that was in widespread use but potentially dangerous was the Bog Hop, Bog Bean or Buck Bean, (*Menyathes trifoliata*). It contains very powerful compounds, and has been used widely in medicine. Small doses were used as a tonic and this particular use is still remembered and sought after today.[25] Back in 1862 Johnson[26] reported that "*Large quantities are said to be annually collected for the adulteration of beer in this country; an application of the herb that must be considered fraudulent, as well as illegal, though, the plant being merely a bitter tonic, its admixture is far less injurious than many to which our national beverage is too frequently subjected.*"

Lest you be tempted, here is what Charles Millspaugh reported: "*Large doses of the root of this plant cause profuse vomitting and purging together with exhausting diaphoresis* [sweating]. *Smaller doses cause confusion and vertigo, pressive headaches, dimness of vision, contraction of the pupil, twitching of the facial muscles, a sensation of coldness in the stomach and oesophagus, followed by nausea, distension and fullness of the abdomen, with griping, constipation, frequent desire to urine with scanty discharge oppression of the chest with increased respiration and accelerated pulse, cramps in the legs, sleeplessness, coldness of the extremities, followed by fever without thirst, and extreme weakness of the whole body."* [27]

Similarly, the use of Tansy (*Tanacetum vulgare*) and Mugwort (*Artemisia vulgaris*) may have produced toxic effects. A close relation of the Mugwort is the Wormwood (*Artemisia absinthium*) that proved so mind altering that it caused permanent brain damage when used in Vermouth and Absinthe and was banned in 1915. Back in the 17th century Evelyn listed it as a substitute for Hops.

Gathering Bog Bean in medieval times.

There is another possibility concerning the intoxicating power of the ale.   Maybe, on occasions, the barley for the malt was contaminated with ergot.   This is a parasitic fungus (*Claviceps purpurea*) which produces little dark purplish fruiting bodies among the grains in the ear where they look just like a darkened grain and therefore overlooked easily.   Indeed it was not until recent times that this was identified as the cause of horrific poisoning, known as ergotism.   If it got into the ale then it would indeed be a powerful brew.[28]

Ale-hoof,
better known today as Ground-ivy.
Glechoma hederacea

Meadow-sweet, Filipendula ulmaria, used in the production of mead and ale.

It contains powerful compounds that acted as a preservative and which also made it a valuable antiseptic and fragrant strewing herb.

It is said to have been the favourite strewing herb of Queen Elizabeth I. It would have been cut and collected in bulk from wet meadow. It is not a heathland plant.

Tansy, Tanacetum vulgare, used as a bitter brewing herb for its preserving qualities.

Its bitterness brought it into service for a wide range of culinary sues, especially during the Middle Ages when strong flavours were in vogue. It was used by the Church at Easter to commemorate the bitter herbs of the Festival of the Passover in the Bible.

Today, there are concerns over the safety of some of its constituents and it is best not consumed.

This has tenacious creeping roots, which will run wildly through loose sand, and so it can be found on the edge of heathlands although it is much happier with richer soils.

BODY TALK

LING FOR HEALING

NB. The following is presented for historical interest. Although much is valid today, readers should seek qualified medical advice before embarking upon any course of herbal medicines. Plants contain powerful compounds.

When it came to health care Ling was excellent for keeping the heathlanders in good working order. Its prime virtue was its antiseptic qualities, which they could make available with a simple decoction. The heathlanders would have used this widely, from bathing wounds, acne, and chilblains, through to soothing eyes. Taken internally, the properties act primarily upon the kidneys and urinary tract, dealing with cystitis and urethritis. Sustained consumption, for a month or more, breaks up kidney and bladder stones. Once in the blood stream its compounds cause the blood vessels to constrict, strengthening the heart and raising blood pressure moderately. At the same time the compounds clean the system and stimulate the liver and kidneys to deal with the waste. In these ways it deals with compounds like uric acid, reducing gout and bringing relief to some arthritic and rheumatic conditions. These were treated by the heathlanders with linaments and poultices of Ling. Had they had baths they could have simply added the decoction to the bath water and gained some relief, which would have reduced their nervous irritability too. It has proved to be good for digestive disorders, such as stomach ache and colic, because it stimulates the bile to aid digestion, giving people back their appetites. Coughs and colds were so treated too. Thus, as an all-round tonic, it soothed depression and, being mildly sedative, offset insomnia. The heathlanders did themselves good, without realising it, just by drinking their heather tea.

The best part to use was the fresh flowering shoots. That limited its availability, although it could be collected and dried for later use without losing *all* its qualities. Knowledge of this herb seems to

64

have been widespread, wherever Ling grew; it has an entry, for example, in K'Eogh's Irish herbal of 1735 *"About a half pint of decoction in spring water drunk warm, is very good against stone in the bladder if taken for thirty days. After which, the patient must take a bath made of a decoction of it, and this process must be often repeated."* It is not well documented in the early classical medical writings however, but that is due probably to it not being a familiar plant in much of the eastern Mediterranean. Even in Italy it is found only in the north. Much, if not all, of the foregoing has been proven valid by modern pharmaceutical sciences. The cosmetics industry has also been interested because one of the compounds in Ling is arbutin, which is the safest, most efficient and effective compound to remove skin pigments. It goes into those skin care products designed to whiten the skin. Does any reader know if this was known and exploited in the days when a pale complexion was highly desirable to distinguish ladies of position from common sun-tanned labourers?

(The section on honey contains medicinal matters too)

HORTICULTURAL USAGE

Heathers, heather gardens, and companion planting with dwarf conifers are all very much part of the garden scene today. Indeed, it is very big business to the horticulture trades and those dependent upon them; it is estimated that fifteen million *Callunas* are grown each year.[29] This is a relatively new fashion for it was only in the early 19th century that garden writers began to record the introduction of heathers into garden schemes.

Earlier than that they had been part of the natural landscape: a place for game and hunting. Then through the 17th and 18th centuries we began to appreciate the beauty of England to the extent of deliberately enhancing estates with the addition of trees and water etc. into the 'landscape garden' designs of the 18th century. Even then, as a ground cover plant, rather than a design feature, any Ling was barely noticed and rarely commented upon, so its use is probably under-recorded. Of course not all estates were on suitable soils but Painshill Park at Cobham, Surrey, was indeed on acid sand. There the Hon. Charles Hamilton had a grand landscape garden designed for him that soon became one of the most famous in the land and was much visited, making it a very influential site. The estate fell on hard times so that nobody altered it. It simply got swamped by invading trees and shrubs and undergrowth but has now been saved and largely restored. The guides point out one area that had originally been a rocky heathery sort of 'alpine' gorge and they recount with delight how ladies of a gentle disposition were too frightened to pass through it on their tour of the estate! Heathlands around London were the haunt of notorious highwaymen at the time so perhaps this was reflected, in part, in their fears. More and more of the heathlands in the Home Counties, and beyond, got enclosed into private estates as such 'wastes' were the only land left. Fortunately for their owners, really impressive spring gardens could be produced on such soil with the massed use of ericaceous shrubs (Rhododendrons, Azaleas, etc.) The season of colour was extended with *Calluna* and *Erica*. Such developments were powered at this time by the introduction of hundreds of new species from abroad. North America was still yielding new material but even more came from the East with the opening up of China and Japan. It was soon found that species from East and West would hybridize successfully. It was possible to build up impressive collections very fast and many great families, such as the Rothschilds, did just that. The Duke of Gloucester held Bagshot Park, visited by the influential horticultural writer John Claudius Loudon in 1828 and again in 1829. He reported,

"The scene that struck us with most force during this visit was the American ground, in which the tufted masses of peat-earth shrubs, magnolias, rhododendrons, andromedas, azaleas, kalmias, ericas[30] &c., looked admirably."[31]

Obviously there were many nurserymen working to supply demand. The group of them turned the great heathlands of West Surrey into the world centre for such produce. The first of note was the Knaphill nursery, which claimed on its catalogues in the 1930s that it was founded in 1760, but Eleanor Willson was unable trace documentation to verify this.[32] Next came the Goldsworth Nursery. Again there is no certain date but the 1790s is favoured by Willson. Thirdly, Jackman's nursery started in 1810. Theirs was a remote site. Modern Woking didn't exist, as the railway was yet to come, but there were two waterways - the Basingstoke Canal and the Wey Navigation. In the early days most of the produce had to be carted so the coming of the railway was a great boon, especially as it linked with Southampton docks for overseas trade.

This planting style had become fashionable rapidly and lasted right through to Edwardian times, when the last venture on a grand scale was the creation of the Valley Garden and Savil Garden in Windsor Great Park. The foremost garden writer of the time was Gertrude Jekyll, who in 1900 published her influential *Home and Garden* in which she describes the planting of a bank of brier roses, saying she would clothe the whole bank with our wild heathers, with a predominance of *Calluna*.

"My Brier Rose garden should have grass paths; whether wide or narrow, straight or winding, could only be determined on the spot

and in relation to all that was near about it. It is one of the few kinds of gardening that could be easily done on such poor sandy soil as mine, because its hungry dryness suits the companion Cistuses and also the setting of wild Heaths which should be mingled with the fine grasses natural to the heathy soil."

"When I advised the planting the planting of the common Heath (Calluna) as the groundwork of the Briers, it was with no thought of its flowering, for that is not till August, but for the sake of its quiet leaf-colouring; grey green when the Briers bloom, and later of a sober rustiness; its own change of colouring keeping pace with that of the small Rose bushes. In neither case do the companion plants imitate or match each other in colour, but both advance in the progress of the year's transformation by such a sequence of quiet harmonies, that at every season each is the better for the nearness of the other."

"There are so many beautiful kinds that it is hard to resist getting a larger number of varieties that look well together." Nevertheless she urges restraint and preferred *"the wild Calluna to be in chief abundance......for the sake of its quiet leaf colouring."* [33]

If she had known what an array of different *Calluna* cultivars would be available a hundred years later she would have been quite astonished. Today the market is very different. There were 1,713 different *Callunas* listed on the International Register when the *Heathland Harvest* was published in 1997. Now, for this version, the total has risen to 2135. However, of these only 654 have been validly published and described; the others are either early names, or synonyms, or have not yet been fully accepted.[34] Even so, 654 is quite remarkable when it is remembered that the genus *Calluna* has only one species in it. Consequently it is not possible to breed new cultivars by hybridizing one closely related species with another, as is the normal practice with so many thousands of our garden plants. Instead today's great variety has been built up gradually from natural mutations and genetic variations spotted wild in the countryside and in more recent times in the nurseries of our growers. These are then propagated from cuttings to retain their particular and desirable characteristics. Some carry their origins in their cultivar name, and take us straight to the southern heathlands, such as 'Kynance' from the Cornish cove of that name. Others introduce us to the original enthusiasts, such as 'Mrs Ronald Gray' found by her husband on the cliff edge in Devon in 1933; he has a cultivar of the Irish *Erica mackaiana* named after him.

There is already a natural range of colours on most heathlands to the eye of anyone attuned to subtle variations through the harmonies of pinks and mauves, even white if you are very lucky. Many people associate 'lucky white heather' with Scotland but this is not a reflection of its natural distribution; it's worth looking out for a white sprig on any heathland. The notion of white heather being 'lucky' appears to be of 19th century origin. An important contribution was made that century when the gardener of Sir Charles Lemon spotted a double flowered Ling, which was brought back and grown in Lemon's garden for many years. It was given the name *Calluna vulgaris flore plena* and in 1929 was granted the Royal Horticultural Society's Award of Merit (although no longer valid since changes to the system). It is still available and has been joined by another lovely pink double named after 'J. H. Hamilton' who was at one time a partner in the Maxwell & Beale nursery. It came from Yorkshire rather than the southern heathlands but that famous nursery did market several heathers of southern origin. From Broadstone Moor in Dorset came 'Mrs Pat' in 1925 - found by and named after the wife of the nursery manager P. S. Patrick. In 1926 an unknown lady walking her dog in the New Forest found another fine variation and sent three cuttings to the nursery of which two rooted and so in 1928 the nursery introduced the famous 'H. E. Beale'. Their 'Mullion' came from Mullion Cove in Cornwall in 1923.

Cornish heathland has been a good source of all the heathers. Around 1929 a Miss Moseley found a tiny grey foliaged *Calluna* growing in a crevice of the serpentine rock near the Lizard. She gave it to Walter Ingwersen, founder of the famous nursery of that name, to propagate and in due course it was given the pet name of the lady's sister and marketed as 'Sister Anne'; she was, incidentally, also a nurse. That same great plantsman has 'Walter Ingwersen' named

after him. He collected the original material in 1928 from the Minho Mountains of Portugal. It was a valuable addition not only for its exceptionally long lilac flower spikes but also because it extended the colour season in the garden by flowering very late. He named it 'Elegantissima' only to have that disallowed because it was already in use for a Dutch cultivar, so it was named after him instead. It did not prove fully hardy and so is now extinct, succeeded by later grey-leaved discoveries.

Cornwall also provided material for the Foxhollow Nursery, whose John F. Letts found 'Moushole' in the Penzance area about 1965. Their good spreading cultivar, 'Foxhollow Wanderer' was found growing over one of the old Cornish copper mines.

The above are just a few of the many cultivars originating in the southern heaths, selected here because they have stood the test of time and are still available commercially.[35] Do not, however, let the foregoing encourage you to uproot our wild plants; *Calluna* can be propagated very successfully from just one tiny cutting, but even the taking of that is illegal on many sites, such as National Trust properties.

BAD NEWS!

It is all very well exploring the virtues of the various heathers out on the heathlands but did things ever go wrong? On the whole these are very tough shrubs and so notions akin to 'crop failure' do not arise often. Fire is always a threat and more so now than in the past. Late spring frosts over the cold heathland soils are a more regular hazard. These burn off the new shoots and can thereby retard the heather for the season. Otherwise there are two organisms worth considering.

There is a little dark brown Heather Beetle that can wreak havoc with Ling. The shrub has to take the full impact because this beetle is the only invertebrate on the heathlands that is dependent entirely upon Ling through all stages of its life. Its populations are cyclical and when numbers build up, the larvae feeding on the new shoots are so destructive that they can actually kill the plant. This is noticeably so if an attack coincides with a period of drought that retards regeneration. Obviously on a small heath where there was pressure to provide enough fuel turf and grazing this could be serious. Unfortunately we do not know enough about the history of the beetle. Today it is more of a problem on the northern moorland Ling, affecting grouse rearing, than it is on the southern heathlands. Has that always been the case? Some people think that the beetle has advantages in that it provokes the Ling to regenerate from lower down the stems or from the rootstock. Without that regeneration there is the opportunity for other invasive species, such as grasses, to move in - good news if you want grazing but bad news if you want turf. Interestingly, modern studies show that an increase in nitrogen levels promotes an increase in beetle numbers. Nitrogen pollution is a concern for the southern heathlands since thousands of tonnes are rained down on the land every year from car and plane emissions. There is also a risk of pollution from nitrogen fertilizers on adjacent farmland. These problems would not have occurred in the past. We do know there must have been plenty of these beetles around because there is a species of wasp that has evolved to parasitize them; when beetle numbers increase so do the wasps and they are very effective in knocking back the beetle population.[36]

Another parasite about which we know very little is a plant: the Dodder (*Cuscuta epithymum et al.*). It will parasitize Ling and Furze, although it is much more difficult to find on the latter (it is shown on furze for the 6p postage stamp for Alderney in the Channel Islands). It produces a gauze of reddish stems bobbled with tiny heads of pink flowers can be quite eye-catching in high summer when it's had a chance to bulk up. This is a true parasite. There are no leaves, not even 'seed leaves' or cotyledons inside its seeds. All it has in its seeds is a minute coil of stem, which bursts out when the temperature and moisture are right. This minute stem waves around to find a suitable host and then it's off. Failure to find a host stem within reach results in death so look for Dodder where the heather is a carpet of thick short juicy young shoots. It has to be quick to find a host as it has no roots to find its own moisture. Instead its roots have become modified suckers (haustoria) along its stem which it forces into the host's stem and sucks out all the food it wants. Its leaves are now nothing more than tiny scale-like bumps on the stems.

Most of the documentation concerns the damage it caused to field crops but it is never going to be possible to sort out the history of this plant because there are several closely related species, which were not differentiated in the old records. Furthermore, ambiguities arise when they were recorded as per their host plant, such as Clover Dodder, Flax Dodder or Hop Dodder, when in some cases the individual species can be found on more than one host. Just to complicate matters, the seeds got imported as an adulterant of consignments of the host's seeds. In one test, early in the 20th century, a pound of Clover seeds contained 18,000 seeds of European Clover Dodder and 7,300 seeds of Chilean Dodder. This state of affairs was finally overcome with herbicides, seed dressings, and improved techniques of seed cleaning. Before that, its prevalence gave rise to such evocative names as Hellbind, Hellweed, Red Tangle and Strangleweed. The Dodders have been around a long time: the early farmers of the Neolithic and Bronze Ages had Dodder in their crops. Now it is often on the heathlands that this weird and fascinating plant finds a safe refuge.[37]

As for its virtues, these seem to be limited to medicines and statements in the 19th century that it was *not* used in medicine are difficult to accept when famous herbals like Culpeper's and K'Eogh's had been promoting it. It features in the *Materia Medica* of Dioscorides from the 1st century CE. The fact that its appearance was blamed on the Devil should not have barred it from medicinal use; other important medicines have come from 'satanic' herbs. Local names for Dodder have included Clover Devil, Devil's Guts, Devil's Net and Devil's Thread. The name Dodder itself has been in use since the 13th century but its meaning is lost to us; perhaps it had something to do with its frailty and thereby gave rise to 'dodderer' for a frail person. Maybe there *was* a problem over using it in medicine since Culpeper chose his entry for Dodder as appropriate for one of his famous defences - *"Sympathy and antipathy are two hinges upon which the whole model of physic turns; and that physician that minds them not, is like a door off from the hooks, more like to do a man mischief than to secure him."*

One of its prime uses has been as a diuretic and therefore valued for kidney and urinary problems and their obstructions. It was said to open the gall bladder and be good against jaundice, and also for liver and spleen. Use too much and it's purgative, or as K'Eogh put it in his Irish herbal, *"a good cleanser"*. Purging the blood was considered vital, even for mental problems as highlighted by Culpeper who said Dodder was *"accounted the most effectual for melancholy diseases of the head and brain, and also for the trembling of the heart, faintings and swoonings."*

Although not usually listed for feverish conditions, Culpeper lists it for agues "in children", which is unusual in itself as so rarely in the old herbals did children get special consideration let alone reduced dosages. More often it was used in both Britain and Ireland against scabies and other skin conditions. These were called the *scald*, giving rise to Dodder being called Scaldweed or simply Scald. The suggestion that these names derive from a supposed scalded appearance that Dodder gave to infected crops isn't very convincing, especially when other European names, such as the German *Grind* (scabies), refer to skin conditions too.[38]

Few poisonous plants grow on the heathlands but Dodder may be one of them. Cooper and Johnson reported that *"Dodder poisoning has not been reported from Britain."* It may have gone unreported of course and some cases of poisoning may not have been linked with Dodder. In Russia it has caused chronic poisoning, with horses said to be the most susceptible. It is tempting to wonder whether Dodder was far more common when the Ling and Furze were cropped and therefore found more often in juvenile growth state that would suit the parasite. We don't know whether villagers resorted to trying to rake it out; we don't know whether Dodder was one of the reasons for firing areas of heathland on occasion; we don't know whether the cowherds and shepherds kept their livestock away from infected areas. All three measures could well have been practised from time to time from place to place but there does not seem to have been widespread concern about it.

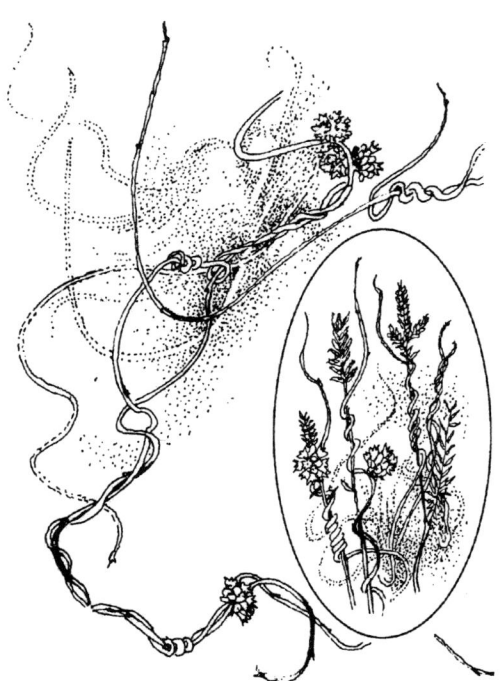

The final word goes to John Pechey whose hatred of a noxious arable weed makes it sound quite appealing! *"This fawning Parasite, and ungrateful Guest, hugs the Herb it hangs upon, with its long Threads, and reddish Twigs; and so closely embraces it, that at length it defrauds the hospitable Herb of its Nourishment, and destroys it by treacherous Embraces."*

The Compleat Herbal of Physical Plants; 1694

THE ERICAS

When late summer sprawls over a dry sunny bank ablaze with purple Bell Heather and hummocks of bright gold Dwarf Furze then we can enjoy the most vibrant of colour schemes occurring naturally in the southern counties today. The Bell Heather (*Erica cinerea*) will flourish on hot dry sandy banks and slopes. It can be the dominant plant, making very vibrant swathes when in full bloom. Where water gathers over hard pans then the Cross-leaved Heath (*Erica tetralix*) is likely to grow, with its softer colour scheme, in shades of rose pink. On the damp heaths of Dorset, South Devon and West Cornwall may be found the Dorset Heath (*Erica ciliaris*) with its spires of bright reddish pink blooms. It is not a widespread species but can it be quite abundant on its chosen sites. Alternatively, walk the winds of the Lizard Peninsula to see the lilac humps of Cornish Heath. This is a more architectural shrub and the dark purple anthers against the pale lilac corolla make it particularly beautiful. The dead flowers are retained and turn orange brown, giving an extra colour variation to the heathlands for months into the winter. They are all so different; no wonder they made such a major contribution to British horticulture. They all belong to the genus *Erica*, which has some 735 species in the world. About 90% occur in South Africa with Britain having just these four native species, plus a few hybrids.

To the heathlanders the *Ericas* are rather useless plants. For much of the year they simply added to the vegetation for grazing but they are not even very wonderful for that, except perhaps the first flush of new shoots in the spring. It was when they flowered that they were of importance because they are a rich source of nectar for making honey and therefore beeswax. The honey is regarded as a fine tonic, good for the heart and nerves and for nervous depression. The high mineral content makes it nutritive too. Otherwise there is nothing extra to add on those topics to what has been said already for *Calluna*, except a reminder that *Erica* produces a liquid honey (as opposed to the unique thixotropic jelly of *Calluna*) and is therefore marketed as 'flower honey'. The term 'heather honey' should be restricted in use to the product from *Calluna*.

Medicinal uses were the ones that have brought the Ericas to notice; the very name comes from the Greek 'ereiko' meaning to break, because a leaf infusion was reputed to break bladder stones. That does not seem to have been exploited much in Britain where tea has been more important: just 3-4 flowering tops in hot water, for stomach ache, general debility, lack of appetite and lack of sleep. A much stronger brew has been used for coughs.

Records for other uses include bedding, brewing ale, dyes (dark green and purple), tanning and thatching but many of these uses do not get recorded until later times and appear to have been largely restricted to Scotland, Ireland, and high English moorland. These are places with a range of plants that is more restricted than in the southern counties, where better climate and soils provided alternative resources that were better for the intended purposes. A few scant records do not really tell us what was commonplace. It is possible that back in the Middle Ages and beyond, when many of the poor were poorer and the heathlands greater, that *Ericas* were used more widely as part of common practice.

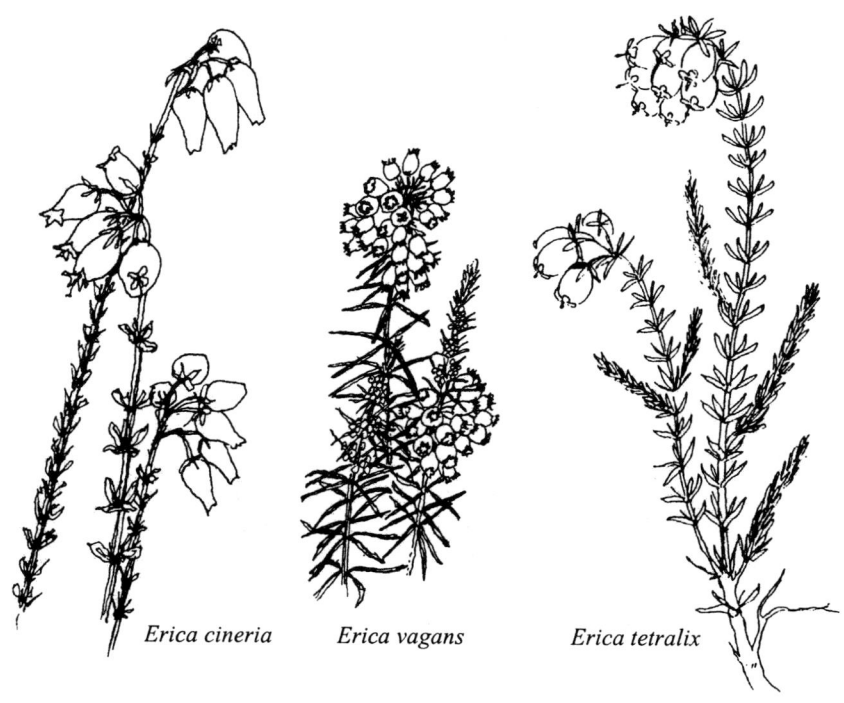

Erica cineria   *Erica vagans*   *Erica tetralix*

The main economic use of *Ericas* today is for horticulture. Many people and nurseries have contributed to this. The Hookstone Green Nursery of George and Leslie Underwood, can be cited as an example. Their interest in heathers arose in 1936 (the same year as they began their nursery, near Woking, Surrey) with the finding of a white *Erica cinerea* on Chobham Ridge. This was marketed subsequently as 'Hookstone White'. Among their other noteworthy cultivars of this species are 'Hookstone Lavender', 'Lady Skelton' and 'Sandpit Hill'.

In their second year a man brought them an unusual apricot form of *Erica tetralix,* which he had found in the local wet heathland and that was propagated and marketed as 'L. E. Underwood', named after Leslie. The next year it was the turn of George's wife, Constance, who found a bright cerise form of the species growing near Aldershot from which she was able to pull off a stem with a few roots. This was planted out in a corner of the nursery, only to be forgotten during the war but rediscovered afterwards and named 'Con Underwood'. Their son, Ken, found what is believed to be the darkest form, in nearby Cuckoo Valley, in 1951 and that has been marketed under his name, while the bright cerise 'Daphne Underwood' commemorates his wife. Another commemoration is 'Ann Berry' who was a cousin working on the nursery. 'Hookstone Pink' is a particularly fine pink set off against silvery grey foliage. It was found in 1953 on High Curley at Bagshot, Surrey. The nursery ceased to trade in 1972 but one of the daughters married John Kampa (who has an *Erica carnea* named after him) and they started the 'Conifers Nursery' nearby, still running today *(on the A319 between Chobham and West End).*

Other early introductions from the wild of *Erica tetralix* include 'Melbury White' from Melbury Common in North Devon and 'Pink Star' which was found in Cornwall in 1963 by John Letts. One added virtue of this species is its ability to produce good hybrids, such as *Erica x williamsii* when it crossed with the Cornish Heath and *Erica x watsonii* when it crossed with the Dorset Heath. Sorting out the hundreds of different cultivars of *Erica* through the years is a major task of the Heather Society.

The Dorset Heath, *Erica ciliaris* (*illus. above*), has spires of bright reddish pink blooms, which has been having a horticultural revival, with garden centres offering grand displays in full bloom in the summer. Standing in their potted rows they do look grand but gardeners need to remember that this is a native of Dorset, South Devon and West Cornwall and so will not be frost hardy in the open ground in colder places. It is not every gardener who can overwinter large plants under cover but keep one stock plant and then layer the outer stems when it is planted out in the spring. These will be well rooted by the autumn, allowing smaller plants to be cut off and overwintered. Youngsters flower more profusely too. Mature plants tend to be short-lived.

Natural variants have been taken into cultivation of which the whites, such as 'Stoborough', 'Storbaye' and 'White Wings', are well worth considering. For a softer effect 'Wych' is creamy with a pink tinge while 'Stapehill' turns purplish. When not in flower, 'Aurea' provides yellowish leaves, while 'Egdon Heath' is greyish green and 'Corfe Castle' turns bronze in winter. There is of course a full range of the pinks and reds to choose from.

Whereas the Dorset Heath is delicate and hairy the Cornish Heath, *Erica vagans*, has firm architectural qualities and is a very fine garden plant with over thirty cultivars from which to choose. The foliage is a bold green that does not look tired in long hot summers, unless of course it is one of the colour variants, such as the golden leaved 'Valerie Proudley', which is grown for this reason rather than its unimpressive bits of white bloom. With the white ones, some people do not like the way the fading blooms turn ginger when the rest of the head is still white but whatever the colour of the blooms the ginger heads remain all winter, which can be most welcome. From the Underwoods' nursery came 'Hookstone Rosea'. In the wild much *Erica vagans* grows on the serpentine rocks of the Lizard and therefore tolerates magnesium, which can be useful on similar garden soils.[39]

THE SETTING SUN

A great tartan of open heathland flung down before the setting sun can be arresting. Sunsets do that. As the sun dies in the west then surely that is where the next world must lie. The ancient Egyptians thought so and so did their counterparts in prehistoric Europe. They gravitated to the most western fringes of the land, that have now been cut off by the sea to form the British Isles, and built the richest collection of astronomical and funerary architecture in Europe.

The great standing stones of Scotland and its islands really do seem to be on the edge of the world, in that silent remoteness denied to Stonehenge by the daily onslaught of tourists. We can wonder about the people who built them and what they believed in and how they used such places but we will never know. Look out over the heathlands and we see still the landscape they knew and worked and where they too stood to watch the sun die in the west. Their landscape is our landscape. It's still there, dubbed "the last wilderness" in the south. We've worked it in much the same way for some four and a half thousand years, not because we have been old-fashioned or die-hards but simply because it has proved to be the most effective way to use such a landscape to answer our daily needs. That lasted in many instances up to the Second World War. Today there are still thatchers using heather. Commoners still exercise their rights to grazing. These are among the last heathland practices. The decline has been a long one that started in many places with the end of the feudal system.

More and more land was becoming what we would call a private farm. The owner did not necessarily farm it himself. He leased it out or put in a 'farm manager' on his behalf hence the verb 'to farm' meant originally to pay somebody else to do the work. Rural work meant farming but even in today's industrial world we still hear that a job has been 'farmed out' to sub-contract. This was well under way through Tudor times but slowed down through the Civil Wars and the Interregnum. After all that, the process accelerated again, culminating in the long phase of the Parliamentary Enclosure

Awards through the 18th and early 19th centuries. Thus no close-dated summary of the history of our heathlands can be written. It's a local affair depending upon the date of the Enclosure Awards for the local manors. Enclosure usually meant the loss of, or restriction of, the traditional Commoners' Rights.

Instead of the old communal system of sharing resources there were now key figures in the locality who became wage-paying employers, exploiting both the natural and the human resources as they strove for wealth and power. The unfortunate lost their lands and their homes; the Poor House and the Work House were invented. Others tried to find a safe haven on marginal land, giving rise to the numerous 'squatters' stories.

Heathlands were now being seen as 'wasteland' in the modern sense and vast areas were sold off. Thus Cradley Heath in the West Midlands went to industrialism. Thornton Heath went for Croydon's housing needs. Hounslow Heath went under Heathrow Airport. Old landscapes became just echoes in place-names. Sites less favourably placed had to find other ways of increasing the return off their land.

Where the soils were well drained and raised above frost hollows, they were ideal for growing Sweet Chestnut which would coppice well and provide a crop of poles every few years. By the end of the 19th century there were hundreds of square miles of such coppices. The most important outlet was for hop poles. The expanding population needed safe drink and Parliament was promoting beer, not simply for its own sake but also to undermine the gin trade with its social consequences. The peak year for beer production was 1878 and needed poles from some 200-400 square miles of coppice. Not all the Chestnut was destined for hop poles. The Cowdray estates at Midhurst in West Sussex had hundreds of acres planted up ready for making barrel staves for pickled herrings. Those estates are still the largest single producer of Chestnut in the country. Thus the high heathlands north of Midhurst - Telegraph Hill, Marley, Blackdown etc. - had their flanks planted thickly with Chestnut where it had once been heathland. All the time these lands were economic the less likely it was that the owner would sell them off for building.[40]

At the same time, as conditions in the capital worsened the City of London foresaw the need for open spaces as 'green lungs' for its people and started buying up countryside beyond the city limits. The famous Hampstead Heath was not among these for this is an incredible survival from pre-Enclosure days. It has never been Enclosed. These were the lands for community use and that's the way they've stayed. It was a battle over Commoners' Rights over to the east of London that caused the City of London to buy Epping Forest but that battle ensured the survival of countryside all over England. Back in the mid 19th century Epping Forest had thousands of Hornbeam trees, pollarded and cropped regularly to provide fuel for London. That livelihood was a local commoners' right. It was ended abruptly when local landowners decided to enclose the forest, grub out the trees and plough up the land for wheat. That deprived the commoners of Loughton of their livelihood and London of its fuel. They banded together and took seventeen of the local landlords to court, suing for loss of income. People laughed. The judiciary was as much part of the Establishment as were the local landlords. They would never find in favour of commoners over their own kind. They stopped laughing when court proceedings became lengthy. The

case ran for sixteen years! The commoners won. London bought up the forest as a safeguard.[41] Elsewhere, such trespasses upon commoners' rights had halted as anxious landowners awaited the outcome, just in case they too might end up funding compensation payments. This halt ensured that there were indeed areas of countryside still undeveloped at the end of the century that could be bought and preserved, whether by the newly founded County Councils or the National Trust or the innumerable local efforts to achieve just the same aims. William Blake's 1804 vision of the "dark satanic mills" ruining our "green and pleasant land" was delayed. Come 1916 the words were put to music by Charles Parry for the "Fight for the Right" movement and we've sung it ever since as *Jerusalem.*

Come 1919 and the Government founded the Forestry Commission with the remit of replacing the timber resource that had been depleted during the First World War. More heathland was taken and went under plantations of conifers. Thus Gertrude Jekyll's 'Juniper Valley' is now given over to pines and larches. Worst of all, for the heathlands, the Forestry Commission set up nurseries to select the various strains of pine that would do particularly well on such soils. They certainly discovered that! The cones dispersed seed onto the adjoining heathlands and wild pines were soon flourishing and regenerating freely. Today those seedlings bear cones in their fifth year, presenting a relentless task to the heathland conservators trying to restore open areas of Ling free of pines.

That said, pines were maturing all through the 19th century to provide images of majesty to the poets, writers and artists of the Romantic Movement. The pines caught the spirit of the age and as the 'cathedral pines' echoed the High Church movements too. Londoners only had to go to the Summer Exhibition of the Royal Academy to see depictions of these landscapes while beyond its doors they were finding the City intolerably overcrowded, filthy and smelly. Oh for a breath of fresh air and a wide-open view. Soon they were discovering the heathlands within easy reach of the capital. Robert Louis Stevenson retreated to Weybridge Heath to proof-read *Treasure Island* and enjoyed the great views south - now obscured with trees and the heathland gone save a few scraggy Gorse bushes beside the main road. Alfred, Lord Tennyson didn't like crowds at all and had himself a home built high up on Blackdown behind Haslemere. The opposite hill attracted another notable who hated crowds - the scientist Professor Tyndall. This was Hindhead that William Cobbett had described as "the most villainous spot God ever made" so surely he'd find peace there. He made a mistake. He said he thought the smell of the pines and the heather breezing off the heathland was as good for respiratory diseases as a Swiss mountain air. People took notice and instead of travelling to Switzerland spent the money building a villa in the hills around Haslemere. It was exploited as 'Little Switzerland' and Tyndall had to build a high solid fence to regain his privacy. By the end of the century Haslemere had become one of the nation's great cultural centres.

The influx brought Sir Robert Hunter who so enjoyed extensive walking in the area that he and his friends feared for its future in the face of encroaching urbanisation. They founded the National Trust. We are so familiar with the name National Trust that we forget just how pioneering it was a hundred years ago. Within a few years of its founding people like Hugh Thackeray Turner of Godalming was giving to the new Trust the Witley and Milford Commons just to the north of Haslemere. He was a local architect, of some note, and could foresee what the expansion of the building trades might do. That can be picked up further west, near the Hampshire border, where in the late 19th century there were still several thousand acres of heathland. Much of it comprised Frimley Park and there was just a handful of families making up the hamlet. Then it came up for sale, ripe for of housing and once again it was the healthy smell of Ling and the pines that got into print. That was in the top medical journal, *The Lancet*, taken up quickly by the estate agents, resulting in boom time for the infant Camberley and Frimley. Today they are one of the densest populated areas in Surrey. Even so, the planning authorities strive to maintain a 'green corridor' down the county boundary to prevent urban development joining up with Aldershot and Farnborough on the Hampshire side. Here too were vast heathlands until 26th September 1853 when Lord Hardinge, Commander in Chief of the War Office, sent a memo reporting "*the next best position* [after Reigate] *for collecting troops for covering the capital and affording speedy re-inforcements for the Southern Counties, are the extensive heaths at Aldershot, Farnham and Ash...I do not believe that any waste land possessing the great advantages of Aldershot...can be found.*" The army descended the next year. "*It created miles of great dreariness*" observed architectural historian Nikolaus Pevsner in 1967, by which time the military developments had long since merged with Farnborough, of Royal Aircraft Establishment fame, and neighbouring villages, to create an urban sprawl that still awaits a writer to sing its praises.

Behind this grim countenance of a public face the Ministry of Defence still owns vast areas of local heathland as military training grounds. They are beautiful swathes of heathland and woodland. Some have public access between operations but the risk from unexploded ammunition means some areas will remain out of bounds. That leaves them as wildlife havens and behind this public face is yet another, far less well known, that of the Ministry of Defence as an agent of conservation. They take this very seriously. Their hundreds of square miles of lands throughout the country are surveyed for wildlife and management plans drawn up accordingly. It is a very active programme, with sensitive areas excluded from military operations, and worked in co-operation with other organisations, such as the various County Heathland Projects. This is a face the general public rarely sees. It is also part of a whole network of activity to save our heathlands, with a dedicated programme from the government's English Nature and funding from the National Lottery. Theoretically this could secure a future for our beautiful heathland landscapes but that depends ultimately upon public attitudes and values. We need the will to find the way. We could be seeing the sun set once and for all over our landscape heritage - or - we could see the sun rise again over a fresh phase of appreciation.

The aim of conservation is not to strip the heathlands bare of trees, as some people fear, but to retain enough to enhance the scene, rather than smother it. Trees are needed nowadays to diversify the habitat for the benefit of wildlife. The Tree Pipit above requires trees as 'song perches' and this species is responding well to modern management schemes. It has one of the most beautiful songs of all birds in Britain.

THE YEAR'S HARVEST

A harvest could be taken off the heathlands and processed throughout the year, as illustrated in the table below. This table is, however, highly generalised. Not all the plants would be found on every heath and neither would all have been needed by any one community, even if they knew the full range of possibilities. Obviously seasonal and regional variations need to be taken into account, with regard to the months.

Plant \ Month	J	F	M	A	M	J	J	A	S	O	N	D
Birch (Sap)	▨	▨										
Birch (Brooms)	▨	▨	▨	▨	▨	▨	▨	▨	▨	▨	▨	▨
Ling (Brooms)	▨	▨	▨	▨	▨	▨	▨	▨	▨	▨	▨	▨
Ling (Honey)						▨	▨	▨				
Dodder								▨				
Broom (Brooms)	▨	▨	▨	▨	▨	▨	▨	▨	▨	▨	▨	▨
Broom (Flowers)					▨							
Broom (Thatch)					▨			▨	▨			
Sundews						▨	▨					
Erica (Honey)						▨	▨					
Bog Cotton					▨	▨						
Shallon (Fruits)								▨	▨			
Bog Bean				▨	▨	▨	▨	▨	▨			
Sweet Gale					▨	▨	▨	▨				
Bog Asphodel						▨	▨	▨				
Bracken				▨	▨	▨	▨	▨	▨			
Sphagnum	▨	▨	▨	▨	▨	▨	▨	▨	▨	▨	▨	▨
Furze	▨	▨	▨	▨	▨	▨	▨	▨	▨	▨	▨	▨
Whortleberries							▨	▨				
Grazing	▨	▨	▨	▨	▨	▨	▨	▨	▨	▨	▨	▨

Sand Lizards are a speciality of our heathland. They like warm banks where they can bask in the sun but retreat into adjoining Ling. They particularly like climbing among the coarse stems of the Ling as it matures. They burrow in the sand to lay their eggs where the sun pitches to incubate them. The Common Lizard (above) also thrives in such places. Both are responding well on sites managed for conservation.

NOTES AND SOURCES

[1] Housed at the Surrey History Centre, Woking.

[2] Penguin Ed. 1983; p. 156

[3] James Parry quotes Colin Tubbs, *The New Forest*; Collins; 1986, as calculating that the average quota there was 4,000 turves and with 1,500 qualifying homes in 1858 there must have been an annual harvest of some six million turves.

[4] Hutchins, J; *The History and Antiquities of the County of Dorset*; 3rd ed.; 1861. Other Dorset info. supplied by Tom Goss, BTCV, Dorset.

[5] Parry, James, :*Heathland*; The National Trust; 2003; p.63

[6] Parry, James, :*Heathland*; The National Trust; 2003; p.63
Other Dorset info. supplied by Tom Goss, BTCV, Dorset.

[7] Trotter, W. R.; *The Hilltop Writers*; Book Guild; 1996

[8] Collier, John; 'On Thatching with Heath'; *Prize Essays and Transactions of the Highland Society of Scotland*; 1831

[9] Ecclestone. Martin; Brit. Archaeology Mag. June 2001

[10] Blomfield; *Deanery of Bicester;* vol.1;110

[11] Liberate R. 244. Henry III

[12] Exch. K.R. Accts; bundle 494; item 7 That documents the Ling as 'bruer', (from the French; ultimately from Latin) which gives us the modern word briar or brier, as in briar pipes which were made from the roots of the Tree Heath (*Erica arborea*).

[13] Housed at the Surrey History Centre, Woking. Ling is recorded as 'heath'.

[14] Robert Bakewell is the best known pioneer and well documented but look at some of the others for a broader view, such as Benjamin Tomkins for Herefords, or Charles and Robert Colling, and Thomas Bates, for Shorthorns, Hugh Watson for Aberdeen-Angus and Francis Quartly for Devons, etc.

[15] *The Apiary: The Village of Budy*; 1880s; Museum of Russian Art; Kiev. See also the painting, *Apiary in the Wood*; 1876; Museum of History and Architecture, Novgorod.

[16] Cox; 164-5

[17] quoted by Heather Toynbee, *Frimley Green: A Village History*; 1985. No source given.

[18] Arnon, S. S. et al; 'Honey and other Environmental Risk Factors for Infant Botulism; *Journal of Paediatrics*; 1979; 94; 331-6

[19] There are many translations available but for a very readable re-telling try 'The Mead of Poetry' in *The Norse Myths* by Kevin Crossley-Holland; Andre Deutsch; 1980. See also his Introduction and the Notes.

[20] For more information and a broader view see *Gods and Myths of Northern Europe*; H. R. Ellis Davidson; Penguin; 1964. She gives a summary of this myth as 'The Winning of the Mead' on p.40.

[21] experimentation with the recipe began in Glasgow in 1986 by Bruce Williams and commercial production started in 1992 at the West Highland Brewery in Argyll. The next year production on a larger scale was made possible through the Thistle Brewery in Aloa.

[22] all Norwegian references in this section courtesy of Torbjorn Alm of the Dept. of Botany, University of Tromso, Norway.

[23] entry 63 in the *Lacnunga* MS. Other entries are 15, 33 & 40 - see Pollington in the Bibliography.

[24] for details see p.31, *Sweet Chestnut* by Chris Howkins.

[25] once or twice a year audience members come up, unprompted by the subject of the talk, to ask if I know where they can still get this from. It is definitely not to be recommended, whatever granny used to say.

[26] C. P. Johnson; *The Useful plants of Great Britain*; Hardwicke; 1862

[27] Charles F. Millspaugh; *American Medicinal Plants*; 1892. Dover ed. used

[28] Additional information for this section provided kindly by Torbjorn Alm of the Dept. of Botany, University of Tromso, Norway. See his 'Ales, beer and other Viking Beverages - some notes based on Norwegian Ethnobotany' in the *Yearbook* of the Heather Society; 2003; 37-44

[29] Statistics in this section provided by the Heather Scoiety.

[30] by ericas he could be including *Calluna* which at one time was named *Erica vulgaris.*

[31] from the 1829 visit. From *In Search of English Gardens: The Travels of John Claudius Loudon and his Wife Jane*; ed. Priscilla Boniface; Lennard Publishing; 1987; p.31.

[32] see E. J. Willson's *Nurserymen of the World: The Nursery Gardens of Woking and North-West Surrey and the Plants Introduced by Them*; Willson; 1989.

[33] Chapter VII; Macmillan, 1984 ed.

[34] updated statistics provided kindly May 2004 by Daphne Everett, The Heather Society, on behalf of the President, David Small.

[35] Information on the cultivars generously provided by Daphne Everett of the Heather Society.

[36] for agricultural information see H.C.Long, *Weeds of Arable Land,* Min. of Agriculture and Food Bulletin 108; HMSO, 1938

[37] for agricultural information see H.C.Long, *Weeds of Arable Land,* Min. of Agriculture and Food Bulletin 108; HMSO 1938

[38] There are several Internet sites offering Dodder medicines. Some at least should be treated with caution. The active constituents are hydroxycinnamic acid and the flavonoids kaempferol and quercetin.

[39] Information on Hookstone Green Nursery courtesy Daphne Everett, The Heather Society).

[39] Information courtesy of James Parry

[40] see *Sweet Chestnut: History, Landscape, People*; Chris Howkins; 2003

[41] more detail in *Searching for Hornbeam*; Chris Howkins and Nicholas Sampson; 2000

ADDITIONAL SELECT BIBLIOGRAPHY

AUBREY, John, *Natural History and Antiquities of the County of Surrey;* 1718-19, Repr. 1975, Kohler & Coombes, Dorking.

BOTTOMLEY, Frank; *The Abbey Explorer's Guide;* Kaye & Wars; 1981

BULLOCK, J.M., and N.R. Webb. 1995. Responses to severe fires in heathland mosaics in southern England. Biological Conservation 73, 207-214.

CHADWICK, L. *In Search of Heathlands;* Dennis Dobson; 1992

CHAPMAN, S.B., R.J.Rose, and M.Basanta. 1989. Phosphorus absorption by soils from heathlands in southern England in relation to successional change. J. Applied Ecology 26, 673-680.

CHAPMAN, S.B, and N.R.Webb. 1978. The productivity of Calluna-heathland in southern England. In: *The Ecology of some British Moors and Montane Grasslands* (O.W.Heal and D.F. Perkins, eds.). Springer-Verlag, Berlin

CHILD, F.J.ed.; *The English and Scottish Popular Ballads.* 1882-89; 5 vols. Repr. Dover, New York, 1965

COLLIER, John, 'Thatching with Heath', *Trans. Highland Soc. of Scotland,* 1831, Vol 2, pp190-5.

COOPER, M. R. and A. W. JOHNSON; *Poisonous Plants in Britain and their effects on Animals and Man*; HMSO; 1984

COX, J.C., *Churchwardens' Accounts from the Fourteenth Century to the Close of the Seventeenth Century;* Methuen, 1913.

DIMBLEBY,G., *The Development of British Heathlands and their Soils;* Oxford; 1962

FREEMAN, George, *A History of Sunbury on Thames;* Sunbury & Shepperton Local Hist. Soc. 1981 ed.

GERARD, John; *The Herball or Generall Historie of Plantes;* Thomas Johnson ed. 1636.

GIMINGHAM, C.H. Heathland Ecology. Chapman & Hall, London; 1972

GIMINGHAM, C.H., S.B.Chapman, and N.R.Webb. European heathlands. In *Ecosystems of the World*, Volume 9A: Heathland and Related Shrublands (R.L.Specht, ed.). Elsevier, Amsterdam; 1979

GODWIN, Harry, *History of the British Flora*, Cambridge University Press, 2nd ed. 1975

HOFFMAN, D; W*elsh Herbal Medicine*; Abercastle Publications;1978

JEKYLL, Gertrude; *Old West Surrey*; Longmans; 1904.

K'EOGH, John, *Botanalogia Universalis Hibernica*; Cork; 1735.

LAFONT, A. *A Herbal Folklore*; Badger Books; Bideford; 1984.

LEWIS, William; *An Experimental History of the Materia Medica*, 4th ed. ed John Aitken, London 1791.

MABEY, R.; *Flora Britannica*; Sinclair-Stevenson; 1996.

MARTINDALE : *The Extra Pharmacopoeia*; Pharmaceutical Press; 30th ed. 1993

PARKINSON, J., *Theatrum Botanicum.*1640.

POLLINGTON, Stephen; *Leechcraft: Early English Charms, Plantlore and Healing*; Anglo Saxon Books; 2000

RACKHAM, Oliver, *History of the Countryside*, Dent; 1986

STACE, C. *New flora of the British Isles*; Cambridge U.P. 1991.

VERA, F. W. M. ed; *Grazing Ecology and Forest History*; CABI Publishing; 2000

WEBB, N.R. 1986. Heathlands. Collins, London.

WEBB, N.R. 1990. Changes on the heathlands of Dorset, England, between 1978 and 1987. Biological Conservation 51, 273-286.

WEBB, N.R. 1994. Post-fire succession of cryptostigmatic mites (Acari, Cryptostigmata) in a Calluna-heathland soil. Pedobiologia 38, 138-145.

YOUNG, Geoffrey; *Traditional British Crafts*; Marshall Cavendish; 1989.

INDEX